UNDERSTANDING The New Testament

R.E. Nixon

John

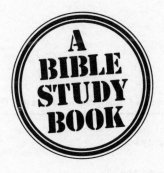

A BIBLE STUDY BOOK

SCRIPTURE UNION
47 Marylebone Lane
London W1M 6AX

A. J. HOLMAN COMPANY
division J. B. Lippincott Company
Philadelphia and New York

©1968 Scripture Union
First published 1968

Published in Daily Bible Commentary Vol. 3 1974
Reprinted 1977
First published in this edition 1978
Reprinted 1978
ISBN (Scripture Union) 0 85421 609 X

U.S. Library of Congress Cataloging in Publication Data

Nixon, Robin E.
    John: a Bible study book.

    (Understanding the New Testament)
    1. Bible. N.T. John—Commentaries. I. Title. II. Series.
BS26153.N58   1978   226'.5'07   78–9114
    ISBN–0–87981–112–9

Printed and bound in Great Britain by
McCorquodale (Newton) Ltd, Newton-le-Willows, Merseyside.

INTRODUCTION

Since their introduction, Scripture Union Bible Study Books have enjoyed wide popularity both in their original paperback and more recently as the hardback Daily Bible Commentary. The continued demand has led to their production in this new format. They are unique in that they can be used both as a daily Bible reading aid and as commentaries for individual or group use.

A Daily Bible Reading Aid

Each volume is divided into sections of an appropriate length for daily use. Normally each volume provides material for one quarter's use, the exceptions being Mark (two months) and 1 and 2 Corinthians and Galatians (four months). Sections have not been dated but where it has been felt appropriate that two be read together in order to complete the book within a quarter they are marked with an asterisk.

New Testament Commentaries

Every major passage is expounded with devotional warmth, clear explanation and relevance to daily life. Most commentaries follow the rather artificial verse divisions, but here the writers have been commissioned to divide the material according to the best exegetical pattern. They thus follow natural units which allow the comments to follow more closely the flow of the original writers' thought.

These commentaries can be used with any Bible translation.

Well Adapted For Group Study

Adult Bible study groups, which meet in homes or elective adult Bible classes of the church school may employ these commentaries with great profit. The Scripture portions are of a length particularly suited to group study.

St. John

There are many different theories about the origin and meaning of this Gospel, and the following summary will indicate only the standpoint adopted in this book. For other views commentaries or reference books should be consulted.

The Gospel was traditionally believed to have been written by John, the son of Zebedee, who is thought to have lived at Ephesus until about the end of the first century. Because John is nowhere mentioned by name (there is only a reference to the sons of Zebedee in **21**.2), and because the Baptist is simply referred to as 'John', there seems little doubt that the evangelist intends the readers to suppose that 'the beloved disciple' is the apostle John. It would seem likely, then, that John was the real author of the Gospel, even if he did not necessarily pen or dictate every word of it. While some scholars suggest that ch. **21** was added later as a sort of postscript, possibly after he died, others maintain that this chapter too is very substantially the work of John. In either event, even if the date of publication is late, the material in the Gospel, coming from an eyewitness, will have as much historical value as that in the Synoptic Gospels.

The purpose of the Gospel is similar to that of any Gospel. It is to present a selection of the deeds of Jesus in such a way that people will come to put their faith in Him as the Son of God and find eternal life, and that those who have done so will be built up in the faith (**20**.31). It may have been written in the first place for Greek-speaking Jews who lived outside Palestine, but its message has gone home to men of every race in every age.

The relationship of the Gospel to the Synoptic Gospels presents a large number of problems, few of which are dealt with here. Some scholars have held that John knew *Mark* and adapted that Gospel for his own purposes. Others have suggested that he is independent of *Mark* and that any resemblances go back to Peter and John who were eyewitnesses of the same events. Recent study has suggested that all the evangelists were interested in the facts and in their interpretation. While John makes the interpretation more obvious, he is not necessarily less interested in the facts. Archaeological discovery has done a certain amount to confirm that a number of things found only in *John* fit well into the background of the times. It is often difficult to know when John intends things to be taken symbolically, and imagination must not be allowed to run riot! But the discovery of a symbolic meaning for something does not automatically mean that it was not also a historical fact.

There are seven 'signs' in the Gospel which present in dramatic form the challenge of the person and work of Christ. There are seven 'I am' sayings which are evangelistic appeals. In the Gospel many people recognize Jesus partially, but only the confession of Thomas after the resurrection, 'My Lord and my God!' (**20.**28), is adequate. One of the features of the Gospel is the divine irony. Men say and do all sorts of things with deeper significance than they realize. God's own people put God's own Son to death. ('The Jews', who are mentioned frequently, seem to be the Judeans, the people who live in the promised land and have a vested interest in the old order of things.) The supreme paradox is the way in which the shameful death on the cross reveals the glory of the Father and the Son.

The Gospel may be divided as follows: The Prelude (**1**); The Book of Signs (**2–12**); The Book of the Passion (**13–19**); The Resurrection and Epilogue (**20–21**).

There are many useful commentaries on the Gospel. B. F. Westcott's is the classical one of modern times. W. Temple has a vast amount of helpful devotional material. R. V. G. Tasker and A. M. Hunter have both produced very good short commentaries. J. C. Fenton's *The Passion according to John* is full of insight into chs. **18** and **19**. C.K. Barrett's commentary is the finest modern one on the Greek text, but takes a generally low view of John's historical reliability. Two books by C. H. Dodd, *The Interpretation of the Fourth Gospel* and *Historical Tradition and the Fourth Gospel*, give a great deal of detailed information and help to establish John as an independent witness to the ministry of Jesus. But no books about the Gospel can be a substitute for careful study for oneself of one of the greatest books of all time. For here in a unique way we meet the Word of Life.

St. John 1.1-5

The Prologue (**1.**1–18) gives us a preview of some of the great themes of the Gospel and sets the earthly ministry of Jesus in its heavenly perspective.

When did Jesus become the Son of God? The resurrection was the great event which confirmed His divine Sonship (Acts **2.**36;

4

Rom. **1.**4). But a voice had declared it before that at His transfiguration (Mark **9.**7) and even earlier at His baptism (Mark **1.**11). *Matthew* and *Luke* show that He was divine from His birth and His conception (Matt. **1.**20–23; Luke **1.**35; **2.**10 f.). Yet all these events were but stages in the revelation of an eternal truth. 'In the beginning was the Word'—long before He took human flesh in the person of Jesus. *Mark's* 'beginning' (Mark **1.**1) is the beginning of the saving ministry culminating in the death and resurrection of Jesus. *John's* 'beginning' is the beginning of everything. If God *created* 'in the beginning' (Gen. **1.**1), the uncreated Son *was* 'in the beginning'.

'The Word'. This would mean something to Greek readers for whom *logos* meant 'reason'. For Jews 'the Word' was the revelation of God's character, expressed in increasingly personal terms in the O.T. 'The Word was with God', i.e. in personal relationship with Him. 'God' has the definite article, marking this out as a reference to the first person of the Trinity. 'The Word was God'—here there is no article since the Word is not said to be the same person as God but to have the nature of God. The NEB paraphrases well: 'What God was, the Word was'. This is the starting point for the evangelist, but in the Gospel story he shows how people failed to recognize the full deity of Jesus until Thomas' confession of faith (**20.**28), which is in some ways the climax of the Gospel.

After reaffirming the pre-existence of the Word and His relationship to God (2), the evangelist goes on to describe His work in creation (cf. Col. **1.**15–20; Heb. **1.**1–4). Through Him everything came into being—not just material things but life itself. So we meet two of the great themes of the Gospel—life and light. The light shines on (present tense). The darkness made an attempt to master it, but failed decisively (past tense). In that fact lies our salvation. *Note:* In v. 4 follow the RSV rather than the margin.

St. John 1.6-13

Vs. 6–8. The first paragraph has seen the Word and His work in the divine perspective. Philosophers of various cultures and religions might have used similar terms, at least, to some extent. In the second paragraph, we come to earth with a bump! For the great philosophical truths have been brought into focus in human history. The drama has been played out with human actors. 'There was a man sent from God, whose name was John.'

The Gospel begins with John the Baptist as does *Mark* (Mark **1.**1–11). *Matthew* and *Luke* give additional material about the birth of Jesus. But here, at least, is the essential starting point of the

5

apostolic proclamation (the *kerygma*) (Acts **1**.21 f.). John is the forerunner (Mark **1**.2 f.) and the link between the old and the new covenants (Matt. **11**.13; Luke **16**.16). In *John*, especially, he is the witness to the incarnation rather as the apostles were to the resurrection (cf. **1**.15,32,34; **3**.26; **5**.33). He was sent from God with divine authority as a prophet. (Jesus, too, was sent from God—**4**.34; **5**.37 f., etc.—but unlike John He *was* God.) John was sent with the purpose of testimony which had as its purpose faith. He was the lamp (**5**.35) but not the light itself. No higher privilege could be given to any man.

Vs. 9–13. The significance of Jesus Christ is world-wide. He was the genuine light in contrast to the many false lights that seemed to shine, and He came to lighten every man. His sphere of activity had to be the world—made through Him (3) and loved by Him (**3**.16) but refusing to acknowledge Him. So in the Gospel 'the world' often comes to mean human society organized apart from God. The rejection by the world of its Maker is brought into sharper focus in the rejection by God's people of their Messiah. His own home (theologically) is Judea (**4**.44; contrast Mark **6**.4). His own people were the Jews, and again and again in the Gospel the emphasis is on their being Judeans, living in the promised land. But God's purposes are not frustrated. The Gospel goes to the whole world and all who receive Him in faith are given legitimate authority to become members of God's family. Their birth, like that of Jesus, is not natural but supernatural. Only those who have experienced it can understand. But there is a human element. The two verbs, 'received' and 'believed' (12) do not indicate two separate actions but, rather, two aspects of the total response to the Saviour.

Note: V.9: 'coming into the world' is rightly taken by the RSV to refer to Jesus rather than to 'every man'.

St. John 1.14-18

Whatever the Greek philosophers might have said about the cosmic operations of the *logos*, they could never have said that it 'became flesh'. This is the startling assertion of John. The eternal Word became flesh—became man in all his weakness, sharing our nature, living and visible in our midst. It was not God taking over a human being, nor the Word ceasing to be God in order to become man. Somehow, in the most profound mystery of all time, He remained God and yet became man. One who was with God (**1**.1), dwelt among us as in a tent, for His permanent residence was not here (cf. 2 Cor. **5**.1). He was no ordinary man, for He was full of grace

6

(which shows the generosity of the action of God) and truth (which shows the reality of it). These had been demonstrated partially in the O.T., now they are displayed perfectly. Christ fulfils the redemption and the revelation of God. His glory is the outshining of the divine nature. This had been seen in the divine presence in the Tabernacle (Exod. **40**.34), and in the Temple (1 Kings **8**.11). Such men as Moses (Exod. **33**.22) and Isaiah (Isa. **6**.3) had caught glimpses of it. But its fullness was reserved for the future (Isa. **60**.1) and here it is shown in the divine presence incarnate among men. This He brings as the unique Son of God (cf. **3**.18; **5**.16,18).

The evidence of John is re-emphasized in order to show that though Christ 'came' after him as far as His birth and His ministry were concerned, He 'was' before him (**1**.1). The fullness of grace was for all to receive as they received Him (**1**.12). Grace was unlimited. The contrast with Law is more a feature of Paul than of John, but he is concerned to show the superiority of the new to the old even though that too was given by God. No one ever yet saw God, not even Moses (Exod. **33**.20). We live in a privileged position (Matt. **13**.16 f.). Jesus has explained Him by who He was and what He did. One day we shall see Him as He is (1 John **3**.2).

Notes: V. 14: the consonants of the Greek word for 'dwelt' are the same as for the Hebrew *shekinah*—the divine presence among the people. The divine glory was no longer in Tabernacle or Temple (cf. **2**.21) but in Jesus. 'We have beheld' may mean the apostolic Church as a whole, but suggests eyewitnesses. His glory was seen especially in His signs (**2**.11; **11**.4,40). There is no account of the transfiguration in *John*.

A challenge: Do we live like 'children of God' (12)? If we, like the disciples, 'have beheld his glory' (14) do we reflect *it? The secret is not in ourselves but in the fullness of His boundless grace (16).*

St. John 1.19-34

One of the most important themes of the Gospel is that of the evidence that Jesus is the Son of God. Here is the evidence of John, whose ministry had the essential purpose of giving testimony to Him (cf. **1**.7,8,15). He was the last of the prophets, but while they had spoken in general terms of the Messiah, it was John who was actually to identify Him. He is the first to give evidence that Jesus is the Son of God, in order to induce that faith which is the object of the Gospel (**20**.31).

John's evidence is in the first place negative (19–21). His ministry and unusual appearance and habits had aroused curiosity. What did

7

it all mean? Who was he? He explains in shorter and shorter sentences that he is neither Messiah, nor Elijah reincarnate, nor the prophet promised by Moses and said to be like Moses (Deut. **18**.15). In answer to repeated questioning he claimed the role of forerunner (22 f.) as shown in Isa. **40**. The emphasis was not on his person but on his message. He insists on directing attention away from himself (cf. **3**.30).

The supplementary question inevitably followed. Why then was he baptizing? For a ministry of baptism was generally thought to be the preparation for the messianic age (24 f.). He replies that his baptism is only an outward symbol and his own dignity is nothing compared with the coming One (26 f.).

The Gospel does not mention the baptism of Jesus, and the evangelist may assume that it is well known to his readers (cf. also the omission of the transfiguration and the institution of the Holy Communion). He does, however, record John's allusion to the descent of the Spirit on Jesus to commission Him for His work, and his description of his own baptism as a foreshadowing of the baptism with the Holy Spirit (29–34). The title which he applies to Jesus, 'the Lamb of God', is of considerable importance and may combine ideas of the lamb of the sin offering, the Passover lamb (cf. **19**.36) and the suffering servant of Isa. **53**. He deals not just with individual *sins*, but with the *sin* of the whole world. Such was the price of our rebellion against God! John's solemn declaration (29), probably coming immediately after Christ's temptation (Matt. **4**.1–11), would underscore vividly His renunciation of any short cut to success. Christ's ministry *began* under the shadow of the Cross. The *promise* contained in John's statement must not, however, be eclipsed by this note of foreboding. The Cross, finally, was a place of triumph.

Note: V. 21: in the Synoptic Gospels, John is said to be Elijah, but this was presumably in a typological sense (Matt. **11**.14; **17**.10–13; Luke **1**.17). Jesus fulfilled the role of the prophet like Moses (Acts **3**.22).

St. John 1.35-51

The evidence which John the Baptist gave, that Jesus was the Son of God and the Lamb of God, led to two of his own disciples leaving him and following Jesus. This was a literal following which was also to become a spiritual following in due course (cf. **8**.12; **12**.26; **21**.19,22). But it was not to be simply on second-hand evidence.

Jesus invites them to come and see for themselves, and to stay with Him. (For a spiritual *coming* to Jesus, cf. **3**.21; **6**.35, etc.; for a spiritual *seeing*, cf. **14**.9; for a spiritual *staying* or *abiding*, cf. **15**.4–10.) Notice that John was concerned not to attach disciples to *himself* (unlike the leaders of many modern cults and schisms) but to Jesus. He could even rejoice in their transferred allegiance (**3**.29 f.); a sure indication of his spiritual greatness.

Christ-centred testimony is infectious. Each 'carrier' has a vital part to play. Andrew's first thought is to share his new experience with his brother. Finding him was, as William Temple said, 'perhaps as great a service to the Church as ever any man did.' Simon (perhaps the name has overtones of hearing and obeying) will become Cephas (Peter, the rock man). Little could either of them see what Jesus would make of him!

Andrew had found Simon for Jesus, now Jesus Himself finds Philip, and Philip in turn finds Nathanael—the Israelite without any touch of the guileful Jacob (Gen. **32**.28). To every misconception about His true origin (that His true home is Nazareth or that His real father is Joseph), there is the answer of experience—'Come and see.'

The titles ascribed to Jesus in this passage are probably, as Temple puts it, 'rather an outburst of exalted hope than a rooted conviction of faith.' But 'Rabbi' (38), 'Messiah' (41), 'Him of whom Moses ... and the prophets wrote' (45), 'Son of God ... King of Israel' (49) are all inadequate because they are limited by the preconceptions of the time. Jesus prefers the cryptic title 'Son of Man' (51). Only after He rose from the dead did true Christian faith come. Only then could Jesus be seen as Jacob's ladder (Gen. **28**.10–17), as the house of God (cf. **2**.19–22) and the gate of heaven (cf. **10**.7,9; **14**.6).

Notes: V.35: 'The next day'—suggests different days in a momentous week. V. 40: 'one of the two.' The most natural assumption is that the other was John. V.41: 'first'—there are three possible meanings here: *(a)* that Andrew sought out Peter the very first thing on the next morning; *(b)* that having found Peter he then found someone else for Christ, possibly Philip (cf. v.44); *(c)* that while Andrew was the first to find *his* brother, John the evangelist, probably the second of the two questioners, also found *his* brother, James. All three alternatives have something to say to us! V.47: Nathanael is probably the same as Bartholomew (Mark **3**.18). Being under the fig tree implies studying the Law.

It seems likely that the preliminary meetings with the Apostles recorded here were the reason for their immediate response to

9

Jesus' call in Mark **1**.16–20. So today there may be other meetings with Christ before the time of committed discipleship.

St. John 2.1-12

Jesus, having acquired some disciples, is now invited with them to a wedding. Cana is probably the modern Khirbet Qana, eight or nine miles north of Nazareth. And the presence of Jesus' mother there suggests that some friend or relative of His family was being married. The wedding celebrations might last several days and it seems as if Jesus and His disciples did not arrive until near the end. It may be that the presence of a number of extra guests put a strain on the resources and the wine ran out. Jesus' mother (she is never named in the Gospel, cf. **6**.42; **19**.25–27) mentions the need to Him as a simple statement of fact. The seeming rebuff was not one of disrespect—but, nevertheless, a clear indication that He would not be 'pressured into action'. His power was not to be controlled merely by a mother-son relationship.

The six stone jars were used to provide water for the washing of hands and of vessels. Jesus' command to fill them is put into effect completely. Then there occurs what is undoubtedly described as a miracle and no attempt at 'rationalizing' looks convincing. God, who is always turning water into wine, now does so in a 'speeded-up' way (cf. C. S. Lewis, *Miracles*, p. 163 f.). It is not clear whether all the water in the pots was turned into wine or only what was drawn out.

The miracles in John are described as *signs*—that is, they have a deeper significance than just the action itself. Here the old flat water of Judaism is turned into the sparkling new wine of the gospel. This has been kept 'until now'. Christ comes as the heavenly bridegroom (**3**.29; cf. Mark **2**.19–22), who by His presence enriches the social occasions of life and points us forward to the marriage feast of the Kingdom (Matt. **22**.1–14). His glory is revealed at other times in the Gospel (**11**.4,40) and the purpose was to bring those to faith in Him who had eyes to see. The majority were ignorant about what had happened, the servants knew and expressed wonder, but the disciples saw and believed. How often we fail to have the eye of faith!

Notes: V.4: 'O woman, what have you to do with Me?' seems harsher in English than in Greek. Perhaps it is best to render 'Mother', with the NEB. Jesus emphasizes His independence from human influence in carrying out the will of His Father at His hour (cf. **17**.1). We too may pray but never force His hand.

10

For meditation: This incident suggests that mundane, domestic problems such as the dislocation of a wedding feast and the embarrassment of the host are not outside the range of interest of the Lord of Glory. Does this encourage you to share **all** your problems with Him?

St. John 2.13-25

Jesus now goes up to Jerusalem, where John shows that He presents the challenge of His person and work to the Jewish leaders. He has just demonstrated, by His sign at Cana, the superiority of the new religion over the old. Here He makes a symbolic purification of Jewish worship as an indication of the coming of the Messianic age. The Lord of the Temple comes suddenly into His Temple (Mal. **3**.1–3). He finds at the very heart of Judaism, in the very place which the Lord had chosen to make His name dwell, commercial exploitation and corruption. This allowed for a kind of 'instant religion' where everything was on hand—convenient for the 'worshipper', no doubt, but governed mainly by the profit motive. True religion withers in such an atmosphere, as many, visiting so-called 'shrines', have discovered. The prophecy of Zech. **14**, which had spoken of the Lord's reign over all the earth and the pilgrimage of all nations to Jerusalem to worship Him, ended with the words 'And there shall no longer be a trader in the house of the Lord of hosts on that day' (Zech. **14**.21). The zeal of Jesus for God's house and honour was such that He was prepared to use strong methods to drive out those who were profiteering from the need of the people to have animals and birds for sacrifice. There are times when Christians too may be called to forceful action.

The Jews demand a sign to authenticate His action and He gives them an answer which they misunderstand (cf. Mark **14**.58). The Temple, as the symbol of God's presence with His people, was theologically redundant, as the Word had become flesh and was tabernacling among men (**1**.14). It was doomed to destruction in due course, paradoxically through their possessive attitude to it (**11**.48; cf. Luke **13**.35, '*your* house'). But the new temple of Christ's body had to go through death to resurrection before it could be a spiritual temple and body of believers (1 Cor. **3**.16; **12**.27). As always there was a mixed response to Him and some very superficial 'belief'. At that stage Jesus was not ready to trust Himself to them as He now so graciously trusts Himself to us.

Note: The chronology of the cleansing of the Temple creates a problem as the Synoptic Gospels place it just before the Passion. The evangelists were not bound to write in a strict chronological

11

order, and it may be that John has put it here as a 'programmatic' incident symbolizing the nature of Christ's mission, or that the others have put it for conciseness in the one visit to Jerusalem which they record. But there are sufficient differences of detail to allow the possibility of two separate cleansings (see, e.g. Westcott).

Questions for further study and discussion on St. John, chs. 1 and 2
1. What attitude ought we to have to One who was both God (**1.1**) and flesh (**1.14**)? Do we hold the two in proper balance?
2. What does it really mean for us to *see* the glory of Christ today (**1.14**) and to receive from His fullness (**1.16**)?
3. 'Come and see' (**1.46**). How far does this express the basis of evangelism?
4. In what ways can we apply the lessons of patience, trust and obedience shown in **2.**1–11 to our own Christian work?
5. In what way does Christ wish to come and cleanse our spiritual lives and the spiritual life of His Church (**2.**13–22)? Why is it 'His own people' who so often do not recognize Him (**1.11**)?

St. John 3.1-8

If the Messiah brings a new beginning for the nation and its religion, He also brings one for the individual and his religion. Nicodemus was a member of the Sanhedrin, the Jewish Council. He was probably both theologian and diplomat. He comes by night in anonymity. His questions show an inability to understand the spiritual significance of the gospel. Eventually he is 'faded out' of the scene and Jesus is left talking to a baffled Judaism and to puzzled and uncommitted religious men as a whole.

Nicodemus' approach is cautious. He not only comes by night, so as not to commit himself (cf. Joseph of Arimathaea in **19**.38 f.), but his opening gambit is also non-committal. He recognizes in a general way ('*we* know') Jesus as a rabbi, doing signs and sent by God in some sense. When 'Jesus answered him' (3) it was his thoughts rather than his words. He calls directly for a radical response—a completely new start. Without a new birth a man cannot even see the Kingdom of God—cannot begin to understand what it is all about. Nicodemus probably takes Jesus literally, as others do mistakenly (cf. **6**.42,52; **8**.33). But perhaps he does see that it is figurative and protests that a new spiritual start is impossible.

If understanding the Kingdom is impossible without new birth, how much more is the commitment of entering it! Men must be

12

born with water, and the reference in the first instance is perhaps to the baptism of John as an external rite signifying repentance (cf. **1.**26,31–34). From there the extension may be made to Christian baptism, which in its turn must be linked with the internal experience of new life in the Spirit. Two worlds are shown to us in the Gospel—flesh and spirit, the earthly and the heavenly (cf. **8.**23). Even a man's religion may be on the level of 'flesh'—human effort. It is not surprising that spiritual life needs spiritual birth. The Spirit is like the wind—free, powerful, unseen, unpredictable—but its results may be observed. The power of the Spirit goes far beyond the physical realm to every sphere of life. He both illuminates and empowers the believer. There is no area of our lives where this influence cannot be effective. Let us never seek to limit His power.

Notes: V. 3: 'born anew', cf. RSV margin 'from above'. The Greek word can mean either, and both may be in mind. 'Kingdom of God' means His reign rather than His realm. V. 8: both Hebrew *ruah* and Greek *pneuma* mean wind or breath as well as spirit.

Prayer: 'Breathe on me, Breath of God.'

St. John 3.9-15

The new analogy of the wind and the Spirit which Jesus introduces baffles Nicodemus further. 'How can this be?' he asks, not so much, it seems, wanting to know how to take the step of faith himself, as unable to comprehend what it is all about. Jesus expresses surprise that someone appointed as a theological teacher of God's chosen people should be so out of his depth. The idea of birth by water and the Spirit was foreshadowed in the O.T., especially in such a passage as Ezek. **36.**25–28.

Jesus speaks not only from Scripture, but also from experience. On the basis of both He gives His testimony. But Nicodemus and those like him did not receive it. An earthly analogy was meant to clarify the heavenly reality. It would be impossible to speak directly of unseen heavenly things to those who cannot understand what they see. In fact there is only one interpreter of heavenly things, the Son of Man. His origin is heavenly, He has a foot in both camps, He bridges the gap between heaven and earth in His own person (cf. **1.**51; 1 Cor. **15.**47). Man could never ascend to meet God. God had to descend to meet man.

Not only was the incarnation necessary to reveal the life of heaven to men, the atonement was also. The bronze serpent on the standard was a symbol of healing (Num. **21**.4–9). The Son of Man was likewise to be lifted up (in a double sense—cf. Gen. **40**.12 f., 18–22; see also **8**.28; **12**.34; **18**.32). As the One lifted up was not a bronze serpent but the living and dying Son of Man, so the benefits were far greater. Here was no temporary cure but eternal life as the result of faith.

Notes: V. 11: 'We speak of what we know'. This may refer to Jesus' disciples, and John the Baptist possibly, as well as to Jesus Himself. No words of a Christian are worth listening to unless they spring from inner conviction. V. 13: 'who is in heaven'. NEB: 'whose home is in heaven'. Some MSS omit this. Jesus did not cease to be God when He became man.

St. John 3.16-21

Here is an important paragraph which summarizes some of the main themes of the Gospel. It shows the purpose and effect of the mission of the Son and the reason why it did not meet with a full response.

Verse 16 has been described as 'the gospel in a nutshell'. It tells us that the love of God was the motive force behind the incarnation and passion of Christ. It was a love great enough to embrace the whole world—a world which was made through the Son but which did not recognize Him (**1**.10) and even hated Him (**7**.7). It was love shown not just in sentiment but in giving. God's gift was the greatest that could ever be made—His only Son (cf. Gen. **22**.2,16). It was a love which required a response of faith, a commitment, in return. The relationship resulting from this could be described as eternal life, the life of the age to come experienced in the present.

Light inevitably casts shadows. Though the purpose of the Son's mission was salvation (rescue and health), the effect of it was often judgement. (He can even say that in one sense its purpose was judgement—**9**.39.) This was not something arbitrarily imposed but it resulted naturally from a refusal to be exposed and to face realities. It is something which, like the offer of eternal life, is taking place already. It is even now showing up what is genuine and what is shoddy and mean. Light and the process of discrimination are inseparable. How terrible it is that for some the offer of life should almost become the means of death!

Superficially, the act of belief appears a very small factor to determine the difference between salvation and destruction, but in reality this is not so. Belief is indicative of a fundamental change of life. It involves the open acknowledgement of sin, whereas, as

14

Christ observes, a man's corrupted nature impels him to avoid the light of exposure (19 ff.). It also involves a sense of need, an awareness of a personal insufficiency and the appropriation of God's provision. All this includes the acceptance of His estimate and standards. So conversion should mark the beginning of a walk in the light—a concept which John develops in his first epistle.

Note: It is not certain whether vs. 16–21 are a continuation of the words of Jesus (RSV margin, NEB) or a comment by the evangelist (RSV). As punctuation marks were not used in the N.T. manuscripts, it is a matter of individual interpretation according to the context. A similar problem is found concerning vs. 31–36.

St. John 3.22-36

Vs. 22–24. The ebb and flow of the ministry of Christ can be seen in the movement between Jerusalem, Judea and Galilee. Jesus has made His first challenge to Jerusalem and His claims have been misinterpreted. Now He goes into Judea (22) before returning to Galilee (**4.**3). In the Jordan valley He began a ministry of baptism parallel to that of John. This was not performed by Jesus Himself but by His disciples (**4.**2), but it was done with His authority.

Vs. 25,26. The ministry of Jesus was inevitably controversial, and there were occasions where controversy occurred amongst those who should have been His supporters. The Jew involved here (25) is unknown (some MSS read 'Jews' and it has even been suggested that there could have been a scribal slip in copying an abbreviation for 'Jesus'). The issue, so common amongst religious people, was one of pastoral jealousy. It seemed to John's disciples that he had precedence over Jesus, whose growing popularity they probably resented (cf. **12.**19 and the attitude of the Pharisees).

Vs. 27–30. John shows great wisdom in understanding his role as 'best man'. His precedence was one of service and preparation (**1.**30 f.). He never claimed to be the Christ (**1.**20). His privilege was to make arrangements for the uniting of the Messiah with His bride Israel. Far from causing jealousy, the God-given success of Jesus was a source of joy to him: There is no other success that matters in Christian work today.

Vs. 31–36. These verses may be a comment by the evangelist (see previous day's note). John's ministry is essentially on a human and earthly level. Jesus has a heavenly origin and His testimony is about heavenly things (cf. **3.**11 f.). Sent and loved by God, He speaks the truth of God and imparts the Spirit of God. The response which men make to Him is decisive for life or for wrath (God's implacable

15

hostility to sin). God's relevation of Himself in Christ cannot be trifled with. Our duty, as believers, must always be the humble, self-effacing part of witnesses to Christ. But v.34 has its application to us also, we have superhuman reinforcement for a superhuman task!

Notes: V. 23: 'Aenon near Salim'—'Aenon' means 'Fountains' and was chosen because of the water there. 'Salim', meaning 'Peace', may have had symbolic significance. V. 24: John does not record the Baptist's imprisonment and this allusion suggests that he expects his readers to know something of the subsequent story. V. 31: 'from above'. The Gospel uses the picture of 'up there' to show the 'transcendence' (otherness) of God and Christ. It also shows the One in whom is life (1.4) to be 'immanent' ('the ground of our being').

A challenge: Does John's magnificent affirmation truly reflect your own attitude?

St. John 4.1-15

Jesus was anxious not to provoke a major clash with the Pharisees until 'His hour had come'. He therefore left Judea to which He had made His challenge (almost 'left it to its fate') and went back to Galilee. Geographical necessity took Him through Samaria, for this was the shortest route home, though Galilean pilgrims often took a long way round to avoid it. But, as so often in the life of Jesus, the action of divine providence could be seen also, for it gave Him the opportunity to present to the sectarian Samaritans the true way to worship God. In His own human weariness and thirst He was able to offer them true satisfaction of all their needs.

The story illustrates, vividly and at some length, the way in which Jesus dealt with individuals (cf. also **9.**1–41; **11.**1–44). It has often been used as a pattern for personal evangelism. (For a fine exposition see Temple, *Readings in St. John's Gospel*, ad loc.). Jesus meets a Samaritan woman on the level of felt and shared human need. He begins by asking her a favour, which caused considerable surprise. There was a barrier of race and of sex which would normally have prevented anything but a superior and scornful attitude by a Jewish rabbi to a Samaritan woman who may have been an outcast in her own community. The manner of our approach to others reveals how much we care for them as people.

The surprising thing did not, however, lie in this encounter but in the fact of His identity and the spiritual offer which He was making. But talk of living water is understood by her on the literal

16

level (cf. **6**.52; see also Jer. **2**.13; Zech. **14**.8; Ezek. **47**.9). How can a tired stranger be greater than Jacob the ancestor of the race (cf. Abraham in **8**.53)?

Jesus had to open up a completely new dimension. The rabbis sometimes used 'water' as a figure of the Law, sometimes of the Spirit. Jesus speaks of the water of eternal life which satisfies people at the deepest spiritual level (**6**.35; **7**.37 f.).

Notes: V. 5: 'Sychar'—probably modern Ashar near Mount Ebal. 'Jacob's well' may still be seen. V. 9: probably read with NEB: 'Jews and Samaritans, it should be noted, do not use vessels in common.'

A testimony:

> I heard the voice of Jesus say,
>   'Behold I freely give
> The living water—thirsty one,
>   Stoop down, and drink, and live.'
> I came to Jesus, and I drank
>   Of that life-giving stream;
> My thirst was quenched, my soul revived,
>   And now I live in Him.

A prayer: 'Sir, give me this water, that I may not thirst ...'

St. John 4.16-26

Before the woman can receive the living water, Jesus tells her to call her husband. The gift of God is personal but not private—it has to be shared. She had probably not come to draw water just for herself—the water of life was to be for others too. The partner in marriage is the first with whom it needs to be shared.

The mention of her husband brings a denial that she has one, and Jesus shows (presumably by supernatural insight) that He knows all about her marital and extra-marital relationships. Her sin had to be acknowledged before she could experience the new life of God. There is no faith without repentance.

The woman's reaction is natural. Someone with such insight is a prophet. He can therefore solve the great denominational dispute. Is Mount Gerizim or Mount Zion the right place to worship? So often will people try to deflect the personal moral challenge of the gospel to a question of general interest.

Jesus shows that Gerizim and Zion are temporary local symbols. When God's hour comes worship will be universal and its location irrelevant. That, however, is not to say that all religions are the same. Samaritan worship in many points was in ignorance, Jewish

17

was with knowledge. God's saving actions had been among Jews, and the Jewish people, as a cradle for the Messiah, were the means of salvation for the world. Yet even Judaism pales before the worship opened up now.

God's nature is spiritual not local. He is the living God and seeks living worship. Men's worship must therefore be not in Jewish letter but in spirit (that aspect of man which answers to God and is made alive by the Holy Spirit), and not in Samaritan falsehood but in truth (in sincerity which depends on the reality of God's revelation in Christ). As she does not understand, the woman pushes off the challenge until later, when the Messiah comes. Back comes the startling reply: 'I am He'. The enjoyment of His presence is still the key to worship.

Note: V. 18: 'five husbands' may refer to the five peoples with their heathen 'baals' ('baal' meant 'husband') who were the ancestors of the Samaritans (2 Kings **17**.24–33). If this were so, it would explain why the woman raised the question of the right place to worship.

St. John 4.27-38

The private personal conversation which Jesus has with the woman has to come to an end with the arrival of the disciples. They are still at the stage of being surprised at His attitude to women, but have become aware that they are in no position to question His actions. The woman left her waterpot and went off to spread the news of her meeting with someone so remarkable that He might even be the Messiah.

If the woman has made a possible discovery after misunderstanding, the disciples continue to misunderstand. They are rightly concerned about Jesus' physical welfare, but cannot appreciate His spiritual metaphor. He was sustained by doing His Father's will (**5**.30; **6**.38) and completing His work (**5**.36; **17**.4; **19**.28–30). Others too were to be sustained (and still are) by His obedience to the uttermost (**6**.51).

In the natural world there may have been four months between the end of sowing and the beginning of harvest. In the spiritual world sowing and reaping may seem almost simultaneous. The work of the gospel is teamwork, and there are always different parts for different people to play in its furtherance (cf. 1 Cor. **3**.6). As far as the presentation of the gospel to the Samaritans was concerned, John the Baptist and his disciples had done their part, Jesus and His disciples were now doing theirs, and in due course Philip and the others were to do theirs (Acts **8**.5–25). Each group and individual is helping in the mission of the Son and of the Spirit. No comparison should be made between the importance of the spiritual work of one group and that of another.

Notes: V. 28: she left her jar probably because she was in a hurry to tell her friends and come back. It was not necessarily because her mind was totally absorbed with what she had heard. V. 35: although this could have been a proverbial saying there is no precise evidence that it was. It might simply be that the scene was set four months before harvest. The fields were 'white' probably with the head-dresses of the Samaritans.

For meditation: One simple, factual testimony led many to 'come and see' (29f.). Does your testimony provoke such a response?

St. John 4.39-45

There is no stopping the testimony to Christ. Despite the unbelief of the Jews (**1**.11), knowing all that they did of God (**4**.22), we see the Samaritans believing in Jesus. This was not yet a full Christian faith. In the first instance it was based upon what the woman had said about a man who had some sort of supernatural knowledge of her life. Nevertheless this was testimony—part of the unfolding of the whole testimony to Christ in the Gospel. The testimony of God (**5**.37), or of Christ Himself (**3**.32), or of His deeds (**5**.36), or of some other person (**1**.7) is one of the bases of faith in the Gospel.

The Samaritans gave Jesus an invitation to stay with them. There is no hint that a stay in Samaria was in Christ's original plan, but He was sufficiently flexible to meet an obvious need (40). Are we adaptable enough to make the most of *our* time and opportunities (Col. **4**.5)? So the Samaritans moved on from acceptance of testimony at second-hand to experience of Jesus at first-hand. It was the word of Jesus which they heard for themselves which brought life (cf. **4**.53; **5**.24). The Jews, from whom was salvation (**4**.22), were preceded by the Samaritans in the confession of the Messiah as Saviour of the world. There is no order of ecclesiastical precedence in spiritual enlightenment. *Prejudice* could have viewed Jesus as a Jewish, nationalistic prophet—*personal experience* proved that He was the Christ.

Samaria is a stop on the road to Galilee (**4**.3) and Jesus continues His journey. Here too He will have more honour than in Jerusalem. In fact, the Galileans welcomed Him because they had seen for themselves at first-hand His signs in Jerusalem (**2**.23). Here is the irony of faith and unbelief—the Samaritans believed without a sign,

19

the Galileans with a sign, and the Judeans (His own people) not at all despite a sign.

Notes: 'because of the woman's testimony' (39); 'because of His word' (41); 'because of your words' (42). The same Greek preposition is used to denote the means through which faith comes (cf. **1**.7; **17**.20). It should be our privilege today to be those 'because of' whom others believe, even if we do not always know it. V. 44: in *John*, if Galilee is where Jesus lives, Judea is theologically His own country (cf. Mark **6**.4). It is to Jerusalem that the challenge is repeatedly made and it is the Jews (seen usually as the Judeans) who as a whole do not believe.

Questions for further study and discussion on St. John, chs. 3.1—4.45
1. What can we learn about personal evangelism by comparing Jesus' dealings with Nicodemus and with the Samaritan woman?
2. What temptations to jealousy do we face in our Christian work (**3**.25 f.)? Do we really practise teamwork (**4**.36–38)?
3. In what lies the greatness of John the Baptist? (See also **10**.41.)
4. How do we see light and darkness at work in people's lives today (**3**.16–21)?
5. What are the distinctive marks of Christian worship (**4**.16–26)?

St. John 4.46-54

Jesus returned not only to Galilee but more especially to Cana, the scene of His first sign. The general pattern of His movement is repeated—departure to Galilee (**1**.43; **4**.43), arrival at Cana (**2**.1; **4**.46), going up to Jerusalem for a festival (**2**.13; **5**.1). Here at Cana He performs another sign. This shows His power, even at a distance, to heal and rescue from the gates of death.

The official was probably an officer at the court of Herod Antipas. It is not clear whether he was a Jew or a Gentile. He must have known of Jesus' reputation as a miracle-worker, so he left his sick son at Capernaum and came to ask for Jesus' help in his desperate plight. Jesus' reply seemed off-putting (cf. **2**.4). He addresses not only the official but others like him ('you' in v. 48 is plural), deploring their dependence upon spectacular miracles before they believe. But the man's urgent need shows that there is faith of a kind in the power of Christ to help. It is an appeal from the heart which does not go unheeded. Jesus confidently assures him that his son will live.

The man took the first step to faith by believing Jesus' word and acting on it. Confirmation of his faith was provided by his servants with their news of the boy's recovery. Natural curiosity compelled him to seek the extent of the connection with the word of Jesus. The discovery that the healing was instantaneous and simultaneous with it brought him and his household to a committed faith in Jesus. For it is His word which brings life from the gates of death (**5**.24). So, in the second sign (54) as in the first (**2**.11), individual faith and obedience were matched by Christ's response, and led to belief in a limited sphere. Is there a principle of abiding relevance here?

Notes: Many commentators have suggested that this is a different version of the story of the healing of the centurion's servant found in the Synoptic Gospels (Matt. **8**.5–13; Luke **7**.1–10). There seem, however, to be sufficient differences in detail between the two to make it more likely that this was another, though similar, event.

The vivid phrase 'Your son lives' comes three times (50, 51, 53; cf. 1 Kings **17**.23). It is better taken as present (with AV and Phillips) than as future.

Some have seen the descriptions of 'an official' (46), 'the man' (50) and 'the father' (53) as indicating a progressive revelation of his real self and situation as he drew nearer to Christ. In our spiritual dealings with people we should likewise find them becoming increasingly real to us.

St. John 5.1-9

The word which has recently given life in Galilee now gives healing in Jerusalem. There the emphasis had been on the rescue from the jaws of death, here there is the return of lost powers. Once again water plays a prominent part. At Cana water was turned into wine (**2**.1–11), at Sychar water was unable to satisfy true human thirst (**4**.13 f.), and now at Jerusalem water cannot make a man's paralysed limbs function again. As 'water' was one of the terms used by the rabbis to describe the Law, there is probably an implied contrast between the impotence of the Law and the life-giving power of the word of Christ.

The Pool of Bethesda was a shrine for sick people who wished to be healed and, presumably having despaired of a cure by other means, came in the superstitious hope that they might be able to benefit from the mysterious powers of the pool. Some MSS include vs. 3b,4 which state that an angel of the Lord went into the pool and troubled the water and the first person in after that was cured. This is no doubt simply a deduction from the authentic text and describes what was believed to happen. Jesus comes to this scene of helplessness and superstition and as always His eye picks out an individual in special need of help. He altogether removes the idea of healing from the realm of chance and puts it in the realm of will. The man proves his real desire to be healed by his obedience to Jesus' startling threefold command to rise, take up his bed and walk (cf. Mark **2**.11). But there is one snag, forgotten no doubt by the man in his joy. It is the Sabbath.

Notes: V. 1: it is uncertain which festival is referred to but it was not a major one. V. 2: MSS differ as to the name of the pool. It may be Bethzatha, Bethesda or Bethsaida. The pool seems to have been discovered just north of the Temple. 'Five porticoes'—some see this as symbolic of the Law with its five books. V. 5: some have seen symbolism in the thirty-eight years, for this was the time of Israel's wandering in the wilderness (Deut. **2**.14). The primary reason for its mention is to show that he had been ill a long time.

St. John 5.10-18

John traces Jewish reaction to the person and ministry of Christ as it was unfolded in His actions and words. The true Light had come into the world (**1**.9), and men whose habitat was darkness rather than light (**3**.19) were disturbed, eventually they were to attempt to extinguish the Light.

If Jesus has really come to give new life in a way that the old order could not, then He is bound to clash with the guardians of the old order concerning their religious institutions. He has tried to show them the true significance of the Temple (**2**.13–22), now He has to reveal to them the true meaning of the Sabbath. In one sense there was no urgency about this miracle, one extra day could hardly have made much difference, and it may be that its performance on the Sabbath (cf. Matt. **12**.9–15; Luke **13**.10–17; **14**.1–6) was a direct challenge to the Jews. The Sabbath, intended for man's benefit and enjoyment, had been so hedged about with petty restrictions, many enforceable by death, that man was shackled in legalistic bondage. But the question of the Sabbath could not be solved without going back to the more fundamental point—the origin and authority of Jesus Himself.

The healed cripple is the first object of their attack. To carry his bed on the Sabbath was against the Law (Jer. **17**.21). He has the feeling that the man who gave him healing has also authority in other matters, and defends himself by referring to Jesus' command. Naturally enough they wish to know who it is who gives such illegal orders. But Jesus had not been ready to reveal Himself and had slipped away, so that, like countless others, the man was ignorant that Christ was the source of the blessing which had come to him.

Jesus does not wish to leave him in ignorance, and after finding

him gives him a solemn warning. The spiritual lesson must reinforce
the physical healing. There is a far worse fate for persistent sinners
than even the pathetic condition of paralysis. What the man made
of this we do not know, but he dutifully gave the authorities the
information for which they had asked. This attitude to the Sabbath
became a main cause of the persistent hostility of the Jews towards
Jesus. Yet He takes the matter further—God His Father does not
stop working on the Sabbath, nor does He. Such apparent blasphemy turns Jewish hostility into a desire to kill Him.

Notes: V. 14: this does not imply that the man's illness was
directly the result of his own sin (cf. **9**.3). It does mean that spiritual
warnings are to be taken from physical evils (cf. Luke **13**.1–5). Too
easily we fail to see and heed them. V. 17: God's Sabbath rest
(Gen. **2**.2) did not mean that the Creator of the world was inactive.
He was seeking to give life on the Sabbath; they were seeking to kill.
There was no doubt which was God's work (cf. Mark **3**.1–6).

St. John 5.19-29

The real issues have now been revealed. They concern the relationship of Jesus to the Father and His consequent right to exercise the
divine prerogatives of giving life and judging. This is a struggle
which cannot reach the point of decision until life comes through
His death (**12**.23–26) and until judgement comes upon the unbelieving world and its ruler through the sentence passed upon Him
(**12**.27–33).

Vs. 19–24. Jesus speaks of His authority in the first instance as
far as His incarnate nature is concerned. In this it is derivative, and
in a sense imitative. But it comes from the close relationship of love
which exists between Father and Son. There is in a way little to
marvel about in the healing of a cripple. They could begin to marvel
when they saw the Son raising the dead and giving them life, for
that was the work of God alone (cf. 2 Kings **5**.7). God the Father
who is judge of all the earth (Gen. **18**.25; Psa. **94**.2) in fact delegates
His judicial office to the Son. With these prerogatives there logically
follows a title to divine honour, a denial of which shows failure to
honour the Father. To hear the Son's word and to believe the
Father gives life on an eternal plane, bypassing the terrors of
judgement.

Some men, like the Jews, have rejected outright those tremendous
claims. After all, no prophet, not even Moses, had assumed such
prerogatives. Most men have given them token acceptance. But if
they are true, then Christ's claim on our love and our allegiance

23

must be taken seriously—God Himself is knocking at the door of our lives and claiming them. Note the conditions of acceptance (24) and compare them with **1**.12.

Vs. 25–29. Having stated the general principle, Jesus now shows that these will be given concrete expression in the future and even in the present. Those who believe receive spiritual life now, those who are physically dead will come into the fullness of the resurrection. How easily Christians forget the amazing extent of their salvation!

Notes: V. 19: 'whatever He does'—the Son is associated with all the work of the Father (cf. **1**.3). V. 20: 'greater works'—specifically the raising of Lazarus (ch. **11**); and the resurrection (ch. **20**). V. 25: 'the hour is coming, and now is'—a characteristic phrase of Jesus in the Gospel (cf. **4**.23; **16**.32). It shows the way in which divine and human time-scales overlap in the ministry of Jesus. V. 27: the Son of man, as a human figure with divine origin, was particularly well qualified to act as judge (cf. Dan. **7**.9–14).

St. John 5.30-47

Such a claim to authority cannot be accepted without evidence. There follows therefore a presentation by Jesus of the evidence upon which He bases it. Again He states that it is derived authority, and adds that the unselfish nature of His motives reinforces His claim to the truth (30). A man's own evidence is not sufficient, and the Law did not allow it without corroboration (Deut. **19**.15). But Jesus has another witness of whose testimony He is sure (31 f.).

On the human level there is the evidence of John the Baptist (33–35). His mission is described in similar terms to those used before (**1**.6–8). He was a lamp which was kindled and shone temporarily, but he was not the light itself (**1**.8). His evidence could have led to salvation, but it was not the real evidence that mattered in the case. The real evidence was that the Son was doing the works of His Father (36–38). This was supported by the Father's witness both in Scripture and in experience. This was unavailable to the Jews because they could not see or hear Him directly, and they did not accept His Son who gave perfect expression to Him. So there came about the extraordinary situation that those who possessed, read and professed to trust in the Scriptures were unable to recognize the One to whom the Scriptures were referring (39 f.).

As so often, failure to understand has a moral cause (41–44). The Jews were blinded by prejudice towards Christ. In His attack on them He had shown that they had no personal knowledge of God (37b). Of course, no man could expect to see God physically, but

He *was* revealed in the Scriptures and through Christ, and here the Jews had a massive blind-spot. They were motivated by a preference for human approval over divine approval (cf. **11.**42 f.). The irony is that those who professed to be Moses' disciples (**9.**28) were going to have Moses in the witness box testifying for Jesus and against them (45–47). When a man is blind to the spiritual truth which lies before his eyes, there is little hope for him (cf. Luke **16.**31).

Notes: V. 32: 'another' is the Father rather than John. V. 39: 'you search' almost certainly indicative rather than imperative. V. 45: 'on whom you set your hope'—they had fallen into idolatry by confusing the sign (the Law) with the thing signified (eternal life with God through the Messiah). The temptation to do this has not disappeared. Some modern-day evangelicalism is in danger of elevating the Scriptures above the Christ, but life is not in the Scriptures themselves but in the One to whom they point. The Scriptures are the *signpost* to Christ the Saviour.

Questions for further study and discussion on St. John, chs. 4.46–5.47
1. Why did Jesus heal some people and not others? Why is this still so?
2. In what ways today are people ignorant of Christ as the source of blessings which they enjoy (cf. **5.**13)?
3. In what ways are the questions about the origin and authority of Christ discussed in the Gospel still relevant today?
4. Do we ever honour but not obey the Scriptures (**5.**39 f., 45–47)?
5. What temptations do we have to receive glory from other people rather than from God (**5.**44)?

St. John 6.1-15

We have seen Christ as the provider for human need (**2.**1–11) and the giver of life (**4.**46–54). Now in providing again for human need He demonstrates that He is not only the giver but also the gift of life. He is the bread which alone can sustain men's souls. He reveals this spiritual truth through a miracle in which, as at Cana, He brings into focus in a single dramatic act what God is always doing in multiplying bread and fish.

The Passover setting of this miracle, and the discourse which follows it, are of considerable importance. Under the old covenant the great act of redemption was the Exodus from Egypt. This had associated with it the feeding of the people with manna in the wilderness, which was a sign to the people and a temporary provision for their need. As a continual remembrance of this redemption the annual festival of the Passover was held in which each succeeding generation identified itself with those whom the Lord had brought out of Egypt. So under the new covenant the great act of redemption is the cross and resurrection of Christ. This has the Lord's Supper as its permanent festival of remembrance. But it also has a temporary sign parallel to the feeding with manna, namely, this feeding miracle. Both old and new covenants point forward to the final Messianic banquet. It would be a mistake to think that the chapter is essentially about the Holy Communion. Rather, it seems to be about the central theological facts of the divine redemption to which also the Holy Communion points. When we partake of the Lord's Supper in faith we link ourselves up with all that Christ has done for us.

Notice in this incident the various reactions to Christ. *(i)* Philip calculated human need in terms of cash, and in the unlikely event of their having such an amount it would only blunt the edge of the crowd's hunger (7). Yet he was in the presence of the Son of God, with His unlimited resources! *(ii)* Andrew was more hopeful. He noted the scanty, inadequate provision, but appears to have left the question open, as does Ezekiel in **37**.3. In the presence of God *nothing* is impossible. *(iii)* The crowd, seeing possibly the fulfilment of Moses' prophecy (Deut. **18**.15–19), were about to respond (15). But all they sought was a Messiah of their own devising who would fill their stomachs (26). Note how resolutely Christ dealt with this temptation to short-circuit Calvary (15, cf. Matt. **14**.22f). Temptations can come in attractive guise, and to entertain them even momentarily is to court disaster.

Notes: V. 1: a gap must be presumed after chapter **5**. V. 5: this is the only miracle recorded in all four Gospels. John seems to have an independent account which illuminates, and is illuminated by, the others. V. 10: 'men' means males. Their possible military formation (Mark **6**.39 f.) suggests there might have been an attempt at a Messianic uprising as it was Passover time. Jesus will have none of it (15). V. 12: some see this as a picture of the gathering of the remnant of true believers (cf. **11**.52). V. 15: when His hour came men did come and take Him by force (**18**.12), and made Him King (**19**.1–22).

St. John 6.16-24

Vs. 16–21. After the feeding of the five thousand Jesus again demonstrates that He is Lord over nature by walking on the surface of the Sea of Galilee. Some have suggested that there is a further

26

point of Exodus typology here and that this symbolizes a new crossing of the Red Sea. The evidence for this is rather slim and it is better to take it as showing the power of Christ to help and guide even in the face of adverse natural conditions (cf. Mark **6**.45–51). His presence banishes fear and guarantees arrival at their destination.

Vs.22–24. These verses give a somewhat complicated explanation of how the crowds on the east shore of the lake discovered that Jesus and His disciples had gone over to the west shore and how they followed across as soon as there was transport available for them. They were sufficiently impressed by what He had done to be anxious to search for Him, though their motives were materialistic (26). We need to have a proper assessment of such seekers today.

Notes: V. 16: they were presumably given instruction by Jesus in order to avoid the attentions of the crowd. V. 17: they expected Jesus to join them somehow. V. 19: the lake was about eight miles across, but this may have been a shorter crossing near the northern end. 'On the sea': the Greek phrase could mean simply 'on the seashore'. The story in Mark **6**.45–51 and the general context here make it most unlikely that this is what was intended. (Even less probable are the 'rationalizing' theories concerning the feeding miracle which suppose that when the boy took out his sandwiches many of the others followed suit!) V. 20: 'It is I'. The Greek *ego eimi* may mean this, or simply 'I am', or 'I am He' (**18**.5). In view of the 'I am' sayings in the Gospel and such a claim as is found in **8**.58, it is probable that there are intended to be overtones of divinity in the expression.

St. John 6.25-34

There now follows a long discourse of Jesus with the Jews about the meaning of the sign which He has performed. This is similar to the discourse in **8**.12–59 concerning the light of the world and related themes which precedes the healing of the blind man in ch. **9**. In each of these dialogues there is an 'I am' saying of Jesus and a failure by the Jews to understand His meaning.

A query as to when He had come across the lake is met by a rebuke to those who had found Him, on the grounds that they wanted Him for the wrong reason—merely as a purveyor of bread for the hungry. He had already rejected this as an adequate Messianic programme (Matt. **4**.2–4). Like water (**4**.13 f.), food is a sign of spiritual sustenance. It must be worked for, yet paradoxically it is the gift of God. Work of this kind is therefore not an external striving but faith in the Son.

27

The people then want a further sign, as if the feeding were not enough for them. (No one depending on seeing wonders will ever be satisfied. Paradoxically, however, the greater the objective proof supplied, the less is the demand for the faith which Christ requires.) Their ancestors had been fed with manna in the wilderness. A repetition of this was expected to be one of the marks of the Messianic age. Jesus reminds them that the source of the manna was not Moses but God, and that the manna was not the genuine bread from heaven. This was to be sought, not in anything temporary and corruptible, but in something of heavenly origin which could bring life to the whole world. This sounded so good that they wanted to have it always available to themselves (cf. **4**.15). The mystery is still hidden from them.

Notes: V. 26: 'saw signs'—they did see the actions but not their significance. V. 30: they depend on physical sight, but the physical sight which they have already had has not turned into spiritual sight. V. 31: the Christian manna is referred to in Rev. **2**.17 and may be alluded to in the Lord's Prayer (Matt. **6**.11).

St. John 6.35-46

The Jews have been looking on Jesus as one who claims to give sustenance. Now comes the startling assertion that He is the sustenance itself. His claim to be the bread of life is the first of the seven 'I am' sayings in the Gospel (cf. **8**.12; **10**.9,11; **11**.25; **14**.6; **15**.1). Each of them is a statement about the person of Christ coupled with a consequent promise of what He offers to the believer. The emphatic 'I am' may carry overtones of deity (cf. Exod. **3**.13 f.). This saying is an offer of complete and eternal satisfaction to those who trust in Him (cf. **4**.14). O taste and see!

The offer to faith reveals as ever the problem of unbelief. Men could see without believing, for true faith depended not upon physical sight but upon the gift of God. The identity of will between Father and Son is such that those given by the Father will be received by the Son and brought to eternal life in the present, and resurrection at the end. The twofold reference to 'the last day' (39f.) would remind the Jews of the Old Testament concept of the 'day of the Lord' (e.g. Amos **5**.18) when God's purposes would be consummated. Christ's claim that this was in His control was a further assertion of His deity.

A claim such as this could hardly fail to be disputed. The most obvious objection to it was that this was a local young man of known parentage. It was a preposterous thing for Him to say! But

28

Jesus stands His ground concerning His Father's calling people to Him. Living experience of the Father inevitably leads to faith in the Son, though true sight of the Father is reserved for the Son alone (cf. 1.18).

Notes: V. 37: the ground of Christian assurance is not a man's own actions or feelings but the unfailing purpose of God. Nothing less is a safe foundation for life. David Livingstone described this promise as 'the words of a perfect gentleman'. V. 39: some connect this with the gathering of the pieces of bread (12 f.). V. 41: 'the Jews'—the scene is in Galilee, but, in every other instance in the Gospel apart from v. 52, they seem to be Judeans. V. 42: as so often in the Gospel they think that they know His origin, but they see it only from the human side (cf. 7.27,41; see also Mark 6.3). Our Lord shows that their misunderstanding was the result of ignorance, firstly, of any genuine work of God in their hearts (44), and, secondly, of the Old Testament revelation which, properly understood, would lead to Him (45).

St. John 6.47-59

Jesus repeats some of what He has said before in a slightly different way in order to reinforce His message (47–51). Faith is the way to life, to be enjoyed in the present (cf. 3.15). He alone in His person can give true spiritual sustenance of a permanent kind which enables men to avoid death and brings them into a new spiritual realm. But the bread must be given—in death—for the life of the world. And the bread is His flesh. It is by His incarnation and passion that the world can be sustained.

There is inevitably misunderstanding not only of His person but also of His offer. It is taken as a literal promise of His giving His flesh for them to eat, which sounds very much like cannibalism. In reply Jesus makes no attempt to soften the language which He has used. Rather He strengthens it. He speaks of eating His flesh and drinking His blood as being essential for life and for resurrection. He describes it as the true food and drink. He asserts that it is the means of union with Him and mutual indwelling. He claims that those who 'eat' Him will have His life in them as He has the Father's life in Himself. He reminds them once more of the temporary effects of the feeding with the manna, and contrasts the heavenly origin and eternal effects of this bread. The language is supposed to be strong and startling. The metaphors, eating and drinking, clearly point to that act by which one 'comes' and 'believes' in Christ (6.35), and through which he is made one with Him. His flesh and blood alone provide our spiritual sustenance. This is clearly demonstrated in the Lord's Supper, but the sacrament is not the source of this experience nor is it the only place where this spiritual truth is realized. The believer knows it as a permanent reality, and enjoys a closeness of identification with Christ, parallel to His relationship with His Father, drawing upon His unlimited resources in a relationship of absolute love, dependence and obedience.

Notes: V. 52: 'How can ...?' This question is not answered directly (cf. **3.**5,9). V. 54: 'eats'—the word is a harsh one almost meaning 'munches', V. 59: perhaps the synagogue lesson was the story of the manna.

St. John 6.60-71

Jesus' ministry has already for some time been causing controversy with 'the Jews'. Now dissension comes to the disciples as well. There were clearly a good number of people who followed Jesus in some way or other during His ministry, for He was able to send out seventy on a mission as His representatives (Luke **10.**1). Amongst those associated with Him would be some whose commitment was very loose or who had badly mistaken ideas of what sort of ministry the Messiah would have. Possibly we can hardly understand the 'cultural shock' on men with the traditional Jewish background of allegiance to the law, religious observances and good works. Instead, Christ claimed their complete loyalty to *Himself* as the repository of spiritual life. The harshness of His statements shocked them because of their materialism and maybe also because of their implication that life came through death. To their objections Jesus makes a twofold reply. On the one hand, the return of the Son of Man to heaven, after His death and resurrection, will show them the true meaning of what He is talking about. On the other hand, they had left the Spirit out of account. He is not talking about anything merely carnal nor is He offering automatic salvation through mechanical participation in a sacred meal. The Spirit gave life and the word He spoke was the living interpretation of this figure. But because they did not believe it was lost upon them.

We are now faced clearly with the issue of faith and unbelief amongst His disciples. Jesus knew who would be faithful, and true faith was the gift of the Father. Some separated themselves from Him at this stage. But disloyalty and unbelief have gone further. The Twelve are now challenged about their position. Simon confesses Him on their behalf as the Holy One of God, but even then Jesus must describe one of them as 'a devil'.

Notice the great place which testimony is given in John's Gospel (68 f., cf. **1**.29–36,41,45; **4**.29). Has this any significance for our generation? Observe, too, that opposition often serves to clarify truth and sharpen our awareness that Christ is what He claims to be, the one Source of true satisfaction.

Notes: V. 60: the NEB paraphrases: 'This is more than we can stomach! Why listen to such words?' There are many truths which we find it no easier to receive. V. 67: this is the first mention of 'the Twelve' as such. Jesus uses the expression in v. 70 to emphasize the fact of their being the chosen inner circle. The evangelist repeats the phrase in v. 71 to show the tragedy of the betrayal (cf. Mark **14**.10, 20,43). In the Greek these words come with vivid dramatic effect at the very end of the sentence. The problems of predestination and moral responsibility and their relationship are found in as acute form in the case of Judas as anywhere in the Bible.

Questions for further study and discussion on St. John ch. 6
1. Have you a doctrine of the Lord's Supper? How does it square with this chapter?
2. Why did St. John not include the story of the institution of the Holy Communion?
3. What was the point of the walking on the water and what is its relevance to us today?
4. In what ways (honestly!) do we find our lives sustained by the Bread of Life?
5. What do we make of the hard sayings of Jesus (**6**.60)? Which ones have we wrestled with and applied recently?

St. John 7.1-13

The clouds of conflict increasingly overshadow the ministry. Jesus still continues with His offer of life for His own people and for the world. His own people have decided upon His death. Jesus pauses for a while in Galilee. When the Feast of Tabernacles comes round Jesus' brothers are most anxious that He should go and reveal Himself in Judea. For this was one of the great festivals at which there would be present pilgrims from all over the world. But His brothers, who had still not come to faith in Him, were arguing with purely human strategy. Galilee, to them, was an unimportant back-water; Judea was where He ought to be if He was to gain acceptance. Let Him be venturesome and dazzle men with an open display of power! Jesus is concerned about the divine strategy. The thing that really matters is whether His hour has come. We are no more entitled to try to push Him into action.

In the end, after a delay in Galilee, Jesus went up to Jerusalem, not publicly, as He did for the final Passover, when the issues had to come to a head, but privately. The people had expected that He would come and there was a great deal of excited informal discussion about Him, though largely at a superficial level which failed to wrestle with the challenge of His claims. Clearly, at this juncture there was much uncertainty, influenced by official hostility which muzzled discussion (12 f.). Both opinions expressed were somewhat nebulous. The discourses which follow show Jesus presenting Himself to God's people as life and light for themselves and for the world, and being rejected (**1.**4 f., 9–13).

Notes: V. 2: the festival was held in September or October and was the most popular in the calendar. It was a thanksgiving for harvest (Exod. **23.**16) and for the provision which God had made for the people when He led them through the wilderness (Lev. **23.**39 –43). To commemorate this the pilgrims erected tents all over Jerusalem and lived in them for eight days. V. 3: 'His brothers'— the natural assumption is that they were sons of Joseph and Mary born after Jesus. V. 8: the apparent difficulty of reconciling this statement with v. 10 seems to have led to a scribal alteration of 'not' to 'not yet'. But it may be that the word 'go up' carries with it the sense of going up to the Father by way of the cross (**3.**13; **6.**62; **20.**17). V. 13: 'fear of the Jews'—cf. **19.**38; **20.**19.

Question: Is it right for any religious body to stamp its authority on a particular issue, doctrinal or practical, so as to stifle or preclude personal conscience?

St. John 7.14-24

The Gospel shows that the festivals were the most significant occasions, and the Temple the most significant place, for Jesus to present His challenge to Judaism (**2.**13–22; **5.**1; **10.**22–39; **12.**12– 36). So about the middle of this feast He went into the Temple and taught. His ability to engage in rabbinic argument was a considerable source of surprise, for He was without formal education in that discipline. What should have impressed them was not the style of His discourses but their content. Intellectually they had to acknowledge His skill, spiritually they were blind to His authority. Jesus' authority should have been accepted as God's authority because His motive was clearly God's glory. They could not accept it unless they were willing to obey God's will. In this controversy Christ appears as the one person completely sure of Himself,

32

His origin and His mission. Notice the practical test which He offers (17 f.)—honest investigation, with the *will* directed to seek God's truth (cf. Philip's 'Come and see', **1**.46).

The question of authority can be pinned down more specifically—those who claimed to accept the authority of the Mosaic Law did not even keep it themselves. They made a great issue of His breaking the Sabbath by His healing of the cripple while they themselves practised circumcision on the Sabbath. Moreover their lawlessness was such that they wished to kill Him. No wonder that He has to impress upon them the need for just, rather than superficial, judgements! It is so much easier to be superficial.

Notes: V. 14: the Lord whom they sought (11) came suddenly into His Temple (Mal. **3**.1). V. 15: the same charge of lack of rabbinic education is made against Peter and John (Acts **4**.13). V. 18: 'seeks his own glory' (cf. **5**.30,41–44). V. 20: 'the people'—they may be different from 'the Jews' and may have been ignorant of plots against Him. V. 23: if a ritual operation may legally be performed on one part of a man's body on the Sabbath, how much more may a man's whole body be healed. There must be some conflict of laws, and it should be clear to all but petty legalists which was the more important. V. 22: Moses gave the law about circumcision (Lev. **12**.3), but the practice originated in Israel with the patriarchs (Gen. **17**.10).

St. John 7.25-36

From the more superficial questions which have been raised, the discussion passes to the question of who Jesus really is. Some know Him only as a wanted man and, when they find Him teaching without being arrested, they wonder if the authorities have decided that He is after all the Messiah. This solution, however, seems to be ruled out by the fact that they know His origin. Jesus retorts that that is precisely what they do not know. His true origin is from His Father and it is for that reason that He comes with the authority of His Father.

The Jewish leaders decide that after all they must try and arrest Him but Jesus is protected by the fact that it is not yet His hour. Many of the people are sufficiently impressed by the number of His miracles to believe that He is the Christ after all, what more could be expected of the Messiah (31)? Their estimate of Christ was shallow, with little understanding of His person and nature. But it was at least a movement towards truth. The authorities accordingly make another attempt to arrest Him. But they cannot stop His ministry. For Jesus is confident not only of His origin but also of His destination and of His time. His destination is one that is out of reach of the unbelieving Jews. They think that the barrier is a geographical one and fail to see that it is a spiritual one.

Notes: V. 26: despite His having visited Jerusalem privately, He teaches, as always, openly (**18**.20). Phillips: 'Surely our rulers haven't decided that this really is Christ!' V. 27: they cannot believe He is the Messiah because they knew where He came from (cf. **6**.42; **7**.41 f.). They did not know about His birth at Bethlehem, which is not mentioned in the Gospel. Others did not believe because they did not know where He came from (**9**.29; **19**.9)! It is amazing what excuses unbelief can find. V. 28: 'You know Me, and you know where I come from?' The question mark brings out the irony. V. 35: 'the Greeks', this need not mean the Gentiles. It could be a term used by the 'Jews' (Palestinian Jews) about the Jews of the Dispersion (cf. **12**.20). It was inconceivable that the Messiah would go where they (the Jews who actually lived in the promised land) could not find Him. Our ecclesiastical pride can be as great.

St. John 7.37-52

It is only on the last day of the feast, the 'climax of the festival' (Phillips), that Jesus is ready to make an astonishing offer to His people and to the world. On this occasion water from Siloam's pool was solemnly offered in the Temple, probably this was an ancient rite invoking God's help in bringing the refreshing 'former rains' to end the long summer drought. Jesus seized this opportunity; any thirsty soul was invited to find deep and lasting refreshment through faith in Him. The blessing which He offered was to be made available through the Holy Spirit, who had not yet been given in a new way to believers.

As usual there was a mixed reaction. For some this offer marked Him as the promised prophet (Deut. **18**.15; John **1**.21; **6**.14). For others it showed Him to be the Christ. Those who knew their Scriptures knew that Christ had to come from Bethlehem. So there was a division among them, with one party relying on Scripture and the other on experience, and neither probably aware that had they known the facts Scripture and experience could have been reconciled! Again a desire to arrest Him fails. The Temple police find that there is something about Him and His teaching which marks Him off as unique. But ignorant men can soon be crushed, without any need of reasoned argument, by an appeal to superior office and knowledge. When Nicodemus does dare to raise his voice in protest in the name of the very Law which they professed to uphold, he too is scornfully dismissed as having baseless provincial sympathies. Galilee of all places!

Notes: V. 37: this was probably the eighth rather than the seventh day. The punctuation of the saying of Jesus is uncertain. It is probably better to follow the RSV margin and NEB in making two parallel invitations and then referring the quotation to Jesus Himself rather than to the believer. The Scripture in question may be Zech. **14.**8, which was part of the lesson appointed for the Feast of Tabernacles. It is no longer Jerusalem but Christ who is the source of blessing. V. 39: the Spirit had been active in the world from the beginning but was not to be given to the believer in the full Christian sense until Pentecost. The phrase is literally 'the Spirit was not'. The third person of the Trinity had to wait for His full personal revelation in the world as did the second person. V. 43: divisions are also described in **9.**16 and **10.**19. V. 50: Nicodemus' visit to Jesus by night had suggested timidity (**3.**1 f.). Now as 'one of them' he plucks up courage to speak up, even if tentatively, for Jesus. V. 52: had they forgotten Jonah? (2 Kings **14.**25).

Thought: Jesus is still a perplexing figure to those who refuse to accept Him at His own estimate as Son of God and Saviour. Why is this?

St. John 7.53—8.11

This story did not originally belong here nor indeed anywhere in St. John's Gospel. This is clear both by the evidence of the MSS and by the style. It was probably inserted by a scribe at this point as an illustration of the principle enunciated in **8.**15. Some MSS put it elsewhere in *John*, others after Luke **21.**38. There is no reason, however, to doubt that it is a genuine story about our Lord's ministry.

There is a close parallel between the story and that of the tribute money (Mark **12.**13–17). Each of them represents an attempt to force Jesus into a position where He makes a pronouncement which will put Him out of favour with either the Romans or the Jews. His accusers, hypocritically pretending to be scandalized by this woman's conduct, were using her, not as a person, but as a political pawn. In this case to advocate stoning would be to usurp the power of the Roman authorities, who alone were allowed to carry out death sentences. To do otherwise would be to contravene the Law of Moses which ordered stoning in such circumstances.

The answer which Jesus gives is a model. He transgresses neither Roman nor Jewish authority. Instead He turns an attempt to trap Him into a penetrating moral challenge to those who were prepared to play politics with human sin and misery. His point is well enough made both with them and with her. Note how conscience works in the presence of the sinless One; these men, convicted of their hypocrisy, soon made their exit. In the end all know themselves to be sinners, and the one who has committed the greatest sin in letter and probably the smallest in spirit leaves with His word of counsel and exhortation.

Notes: V. 3: 'adultery'—only in the case of fornication by a betrothed virgin was stoning laid down as the punishment (Deut. **22**.23 f.). The same punishment was laid down for the man, but the woman seems to have been an easier victim for their scheme. V. 6: it may be that He was writing the sentence as the Roman judge would do and that the words were what He then spoke to them. Any suggestion is pure guesswork. V. 11: Jesus does not condemn her; the witnesses having left, He is in no position to pass judgement according to the Law. By implication He offers her forgiveness but does not excuse her conduct. For she is to go and not to sin again.

Prayer: Lord, make **me** *sensitive to Your presence, aware of my own sinfulness, and help me to 'walk in the light' (1 John* **1**.7*).*

Questions for further study and discussion on St. John chs. 7.1—8.11

1. What principles do we use in trying to decide between different laws (e.g. the Sabbath law and men's need of healing)?
2. How do we resolve conflicts between Scripture and experience (7.40–52)?
3. In what ways do we set up ourselves, at least in our private thoughts, as more worthy of the gospel than others (7.35)?
4. Was Nicodemus' position to witness stronger or weaker by his being 'one of them' (7.50)?
5. What is our attitude to those guilty of sexual sin? Can we avoid condemning or condoning (8.3–11)?

St. John 8.12-20

The scene continues in the Temple at the Feast of Tabernacles. This festival commemorated, amongst other things, the pillar of fire which had been given as light to the Israelites in the wilderness (Exod. **13**.21 f.), and one of its most impressive ceremonies was the lighting of the golden candelabrum. The light was said to be so brilliant as to illuminate every courtyard in Jerusalem. It was a festival of light. And the Law was also held to be light (Psa. **119**.105; Prov. **6**.23). But neither ceremonial nor even Scripture is the true light. It was God who was the light of His people (Psa. **27**.1), and Jesus therefore comes to direct men's attention away from the symbols to the reality—God's own presence in His person in their midst.

His great claim to be the light of the world is challenged on the ground that it is testimony in His own case. Jesus replies that there is a validity about such evidence in this instance because He had a knowledge of His origin and destination which they did not share. Their idea of judgement was governed by purely human rules. He had in fact the testimony of His Father in support of Him, a fact which they could not understand because they did not know Him.

Notès: V. 12: 'the light of life'—the light which has and gives life (cf. **1**.4 f.). This is given not to those who simply gaze in admiration but to those who follow. It was the destiny of the Servant of the Lord to be a light to the nations (Isa. **49**.6). The theme of light is forgotten until the next chapter. V. 13: the argument concerning evidence is similar in many ways to that in **5**.31–39. V. 15: the question of judgement is one of the most paradoxical themes in the Gospel. It was not Jesus' purpose to judge men (**3**.17; **12**.47), and yet it was (**3**.18; **12**.48; **5**.22; **9**.39). V. 17: '*your* law' perhaps implies that they had treated it as their own preserve. Such spiritual possessiveness is still with us. V. 19: 'Your Father'—they may think He is speaking of Joseph. V. 20: the treasury was just beside where the Sanhedrin met, but even so because of the divine purpose they could not arrest Him.

St. John 8.21-30

The long discourse, which follows to the end of the chapter, is connected with themes which have already been introduced. Here are discussed His origin, His destination, His parentage and His identity. The contrast is made between what He claims to be, and in fact is, and what the Jews in fact are, despite their claims.

Jesus speaks first of going away. His destination is somewhere that they cannot reach (cf. **7**.33–36). Their tragedy is that death will overtake them before their sin is forgiven. The probable allusion to

37

Plan of Herod's Temple

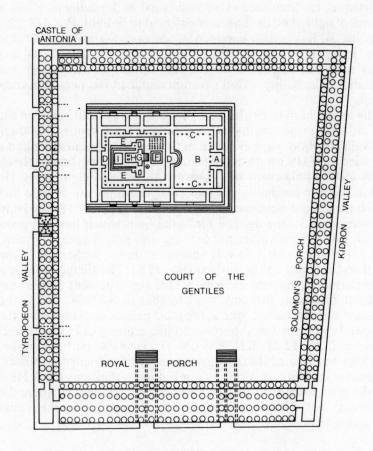

A   Beautiful Gate (Gate of Nicanor)
B   Court of the Women
C   Women's Gallery
D   Court of Israel
E   Court of the Priests
F   Altar of Burnt Offering
G   Porch
H   Holy Place
I   Holy of Holies

death is picked up by the Jews, but they suspect that He is planning suicide. Jesus goes on to point the contrast between Himself and them. There are two worlds, one above and one below. His origin, unlike theirs, is from the one above. Their failure to believe in His supernatural origin is the reason why they will die in their sins. There is nothing optional about the Gospel of Christ.

To a direct question about His identity, Jesus replies that He has been telling them all along if only they had been able to exercise spiritual discernment. His authority was a derived authority. As they could not understand this, Jesus went on to speak of the lifting up of the Son of Man which would authenticate His message. In all circumstances He enjoyed His Father's presence and lived a life of perfect conformity to His will. Such claims, though baffling to many, led others in some measure to believe in Him. Faith in Him should result in our doing always what pleases His Father.

Notes: V. 24: 'I am He'. The Greek is simply 'I am' (*ego eimi*). It is used on its own three other times in the Gospel (**4.**26; **8.**28; **13.**19). Here it seems to carry clear overtones of deity and the NEB renders 'I am what I am', giving the echo of Exod. **3.**14 (cf. also Deut. **32.**39; Isa. **43.**10). V. 25: Jesus' reply may be rendered as in the RSV margin, 'Why do I talk to you at all?' This seems less likely in the context. V. 28: 'lifted up' (cf. **3.**14; **12.**32,34). It already had a double sense in the O.T., where the heads of Pharaoh's chief butler and chief baker were 'lifted up' in exaltation and in death (Gen. **40.**20 ff.). Here it obviously marks an important point of transition in Christ's relationship with the world (cf. **3.**14). Later on, Christ made clear that this expression referred to His Cross (**12.**32 ff.).

Question: How does Calvary show Jesus as 'the Light of the world'?

St. John 8.31-47

The debate moves on from the question of authority to that of freedom. The basis for the proper enjoyment of this most treasured human possession is discipleship and truth. But few concepts are so much misunderstood as freedom. National pride revolts against the suggestion that they are in need of liberation. Is not the fact of their ancestry sufficient guarantee of their freedom?

The assertion of their descent from Abraham gives Jesus an opportunity to discuss the real issues of their ancestry and His. Only the Son of God is able to offer them the true liberty of God. Whatever their physical ancestry, their rejection of His offer shows their failure to enter into that liberty and their consequent enslavement by sin. To be Abraham's children in the true sense required moral conformity to Abraham, and this they clearly did not have. They must, spiritually, have another father. Oh, yes, they agree about that. Their father in that sense is, of course, God. No, says Jesus. If that were true they would recognize God's message which He had come to proclaim. Their complete failure to do so marked them off as children of the devil with all his hatred and falsehood. They could find no moral fault in Him, yet they did not believe Him. Their attitude proved quite plainly that they did not belong to God.

Notes: V. 31: 'believed in Him'—as the discourse shows, they must have been nominal believers. True discipleship is shown in continuing obedience to Him and only in this way can true freedom be attained. V. 33: despite periods of foreign domination, such as the Roman occupation at this time, they always thought themselves to be truly free as Abraham's sons. For reliance upon their descent from him, cf. also Matt. **3**.9; Luke **3**.8. It is similar to their reliance upon being Moses' disciples (**9**.28). Pedigree is no substitute for faith. V. 34: 'commits sin'—lives a life of sin (cf. 1 John **3**.4,8). V. 35: the position of servants and sons in a house and their relationship with God are often contrasted in the N.T. (Heb. **3**.2–6; Gal. **4**.1–6). V. 41: the emphatic '*we*' suggests that there may be a charge against Him of physical illegitimacy after He has accused them of spiritual illegitimacy. V. 43: they cannot understand the *words* He speaks because their heart is not open to His *word*.

To ponder: It has been well said that God has no grandsons. What is meant by this? How is it possible for **apparently** *God-fearing men to be so spiritually enslaved as to merit the condemnation of v.44? How can we avoid this?*

St. John 8.48-59

Most of us are familiar with the alleged marginal note against a portion of a written sermon; 'argument weak here—raise voice and thump pulpit'! There is something of this attitude in Christ's adversaries who, unable to combat His teaching, resort to slander and invective. They cannot understand Jesus' claims or accept them in so far as they do understand them. They therefore accuse Jesus of being a demon-possessed Samaritan. Jesus will not allow them to get away with such slanderous suggestions, for the fact is that He is honouring His Father in doing His work, and it is God who will make the truth plain. Obedience to His word is a passport through death.

Such an assertion settles the question of demon-possession as far as the Jews are concerned. Abraham, the great ancestor of the race, had to die. How could a man like this promise immortality? Jesus has to remind them again that what He does and says is not simply His own whim, for His mission is inspired and authenticated by His Father. It would be false for Him to say less than the truth of His relationship with God. Abraham had rejoiced to see His day, for even before Abraham was born He was there in His eternal being. This is sheer blasphemy and an attempt is made to stone Him for it, but again, for the moment, He escapes.

Notes: V. 48: to be a Samaritan was one step worse in their eyes than being a Galilean. The Samaritans' ancestry was mixed (2 Kings **17.**24) and this may be a further charge of illegitimacy (cf. **8.**41). He is accused of having a demon in **7.**20 and **10.**20. It is only here that He refutes the charge. How easy it is to conduct our theological arguments by 'labelling' people and then thinking we have refuted their views! V. 53 'Are You greater . . . .?' The woman of Samaria asked the same question with relation to Jacob, and the answer given was indirect, as it is here. 'Who do You claim to be?'—literally 'make Yourself' (cf. **5.**18; **10.**33; **19.**7,12). He made Himself nothing, what He was He was by the will of the Father. V. 56: Jewish tradition said that Abraham saw the whole history of his descendants and the messianic age. V. 57: 'have You seen Abraham?' is the best reading. It shows how the Jews misquoted His claim, still assuming that Abraham is the greater of the two. V. 58: Abraham not only died but was born. Christ *is* eternally. Here, as the reaction shows, there must be a claim to deity (Exod. **3.**14). V. 59: By hiding Himself, Christ was, in effect, passing judgement on them: they had rejected Him and stood condemned (cf. **3.**18).

For meditation: Note Christ's desire throughout this chapter to glorify the Father, and not Himself. Are we as self-less in our lives and service?

St. John 9.1-12

While the sign of the feeding of the five thousand had preceded the discourse about the bread of life, the sign of the healing of the blind man succeeds the discourse about the light of the world. John does not record many miracles compared with the other Gospels, but when he does, it is usually with full detail and careful explanation, in order to illustrate a divine truth. It was one of the marks of the Messiah that He would open the eyes of the blind (Isa. **35.**5; **61.**1 f.; Luke **4.**18; **7.**21 f.). Here Jesus is shown in

41

action demonstrating the truth of His claim that He is the Messiah and the light of the world.

As Jesus was going along, perhaps from the Temple on the last day of the festival, He noticed a man who was blind from his birth. This pitiful condition is assumed by the disciples to be punishment for sin. As the man was born in this state the possibilities were that he had committed some ante-natal sin (Gen. **25.**22; Psa. **51.**5), or that he had sinned in a previous existence. If neither of those explanations seemed satisfactory, then it must be assumed that parental sin was the reason (Exod. **20.**5). Such speculation failed to take into account the fact that, while there is a connection between human sin and human suffering as a whole, there is not necessarily a direct connection between a man's suffering and his own sin. (This was pointed out in the Book of Job.) Jesus in any event looks not to the past (as we usually do) but to the future and sees it as an opportunity to glorify God (cf. Luke **13.**1–5). He had only limited time to work in His role as the light of the world. He therefore anointed the man's eyes and sent him off to wash. When he returned with his vision restored, so incredulous were those who had known him that they questioned his identity.

Notes: V. 1: 'from his birth'. He had never known the realm of sight for himself. This illustrates men's spiritual condition. V. 3: Jesus does not deny that either party are sinners but asserts that this is not the point at issue. V. 6: this was an ancient remedy but its use on the Sabbath was specifically forbidden by Jewish tradition. V. 7: 'Sent'—the mention of the meaning of the name suggests symbolic significance. The name was due to the water being sent from another pool. Jesus, the source of living water, is also 'sent' (**3.**17; **4.**34; etc.). As the Jews 'refused the waters of Shiloah' (Isa. **8.**6) so they refused Him. The pool was the source of the libations at the festival.

*For meditation: 'We must work the works of Him who sent me, while it is day' (4). The plural 'we' emphasizes both the privilege of the disciples in being associated with the work of the Master and the responsibility we all have to use our time to the best advantage (cf. Eph. **5.**16).*

St. John 9.13-23

The acquaintances of the man were baffled by the whole business so they took him to the Pharisees in order to investigate further the issues raised by the incident. In particular there was the fact that the cure had taken place on the Sabbath. The Pharisees asked the man what had happened and he gave them a straightforward, factual reply. There was a division among them. On one side were those who knew the religious traditions and on the other those who could see the evidence which lay in front of them (cf. **7**.40–43; **10**.19–21). They decide therefore to ask what the man himself thinks. He replies bravely, but inadequately, that he thinks Jesus is a prophet.

The Jews then revert to the position his neighbours had adopted. This was a case of mistaken identity. Sensibly they ask his parents to tell them. They are perfectly prepared to vouch for his being their son and his having been born blind. But the method of his cure they will not state. Maybe they had no first-hand evidence themselves, but in any event they were afraid of reprisals. For if they were led into a statement that Jesus was the Messiah they were in danger of excommunication. They therefore transfer the responsibility for that part of the answer to their son.

Notes: V. 14: the cripple was also healed on the Sabbath (**5**.9). The two stories have much in common, but at this more advanced stage of the ministry this man is much nearer to a full faith in Jesus, and gives a far more spirited defence of his own experience and of Jesus than does the healed cripple. V. 21: the age of legal responsibility was thirteen. The idea may, however, simply be that he is old enough to tell his own story without their intervention. V. 22: this would probably not be more than a temporary ban. What an eternal opportunity they may have lost because of it! Open confession of Christ is the essential accompaniment to faith in Him (cf. Rom. **10**.9 f.). Tragically, there have been many times, too, in the history of the Church when the issue has virtually been whether a man is cast out of the institutional Church or out of the Kingdom of God.

St. John 9.24-34

The religious leaders decide to examine the man a second time and on this occasion they are in a tougher mood. He must make a clean breast of what had actually happened. They clearly could not believe his story, for they knew that Jesus was a sinner. The man will not be browbeaten. He is not concerned with technicalities which are beyond his understanding. He knows one thing with full conviction—the reality of his change from a state of blindness to one of sight—'though I was blind, now I see' (25). They inquire again how it happened.

Now it is the turn of the man to be tough with them. He had already stated the facts quite clearly. They had taken no notice

43

then. There was no point in repeating them unless they too wished to become disciples of Jesus. The crushing retort follows that they are disciples of Moses, a known recipient of God's word; he is a disciple of someone utterly unknown (cf. 7.48 f.). Yet the man will not abandon his defence of his experience. His eyes have been opened, there is no doubt about that. And if they must force him into theology, into his own simple theology he will go. God does not answer the prayers of sinners. No one has ever heard of the healing of a man *born* blind. Such an extraordinary miracle therefore proves that He is not a sinner but is from God.

But as the man born blind moves steadily into clearer sight, the Pharisees plunge into deeper darkness. There is no attempt to answer the man. Assessing of evidence gives way to prejudice. Living experience is rejected by the dead hand of tradition. Those with a vested interest in the religious establishment put themselves beyond responding to the word of God proclaimed through a humble sinner. 'Would *you* teach *us*?'

Notes: V. 24: NEB: 'Speak the truth before God'. It probably suggests making a confession (cf. Josh. 7.19). V. 28: 'We are disciples of Moses' (cf. 8.33: 'We are descendants of Abraham'). But their discipleship of Moses was very blind (5.45–47). V. 29: ignorance of His origin is the ground for rejection of Christ just as supposed knowledge of it was before (7.27).

Meditation: 'Though I was blind, now I see' (25). This simple conviction has brought strength to many Christians, persecuted, reviled, laughed at or out-manoeuvred in argument. What does it mean to you?

St. John 9.35–41

Hitherto in this chapter the whole discussion has been concerned with the physical healing of a blind man and the identity of a person who was able to perform it. Now Jesus draws out the further lesson of His spiritual mission to the world and to individual people. Not even a miracle was sufficient, by itself, to create faith—a personal meeting with Christ was required.

Jesus had disappeared from the scene (9.12) but had kept an interest in the man, and on hearing that he had been thrown out by the Jews, He found him (cf. 5.13 f.). He now asks him the direct question whether he believes in the Son of man. The man is baffled as to who such a person might be and Jesus has to explain that it is He Himself (cf. 4.26). The man gives Him his trust and his reverence up to the limit of his understanding.

Jesus then utters one of His hard sayings. His purpose in coming

44

into the world was judgement. There has just been a perversion of the judicial process. He will set things right by giving sight to the blind and blindness to the seeing. Some of the Pharisees were disturbed enough by the whole affair to ask whether they too were in some measure blind. Jesus replies that the really incurable blindness is that which has convinced its victims that it is in fact sight.

Notes: V. 35: some MSS read 'Son of God' but 'Son of man' is more likely to be correct. Jesus is still revealing Himself cryptically. V. 38: these words may not have their full Christian content yet, for 'Lord' may be only 'Sir' and 'worshipped' need only mean 'bowed before' (NEB). To us, who know the risen Lord, they mean so much more. V. 39: a hard saying, but all the Gospels allude to the saying about blinding in Isa. **6.**9 f. Though salvation was the primary purpose of His coming (**3.**17), judgement was its inevitable consequence and so could be said in one sense to be its purpose. 'Those who see' are those who have some understanding of spiritual truth which they regard as sufficient, and so they fail to see the true message of the Gospel.

Questions for further study and discussion on St. John chs. 8.12—9.41

1. How has Christ's claim to be the Light of the World been fulfilled in human history (**8.**12)?
2. How does the truth make us free (**8.**31 f.)? Is your life demonstrating freedom as one of its characteristics?
3. How much does Christ's claim to pre-existence affect our attitude towards Him (**8.**58)?
4. If men are spiritually 'born blind' (**9.**1) how do we try to deal with this fact in evangelism?
5. 'Would *you* teach *us*?' (**9.**34). What occasions arise when we, at least in heart, take this attitude?

St. John 10.1-10

Chapter divisions in the Bible can be misleading. While in a sense the story of the man born blind is rounded off at the end of ch. **9,** there is no evidence that the evangelist intended a break there. The blind man and the Pharisees are mentioned again in ch. **10,** and, while the main figure changes from light and darkness to the shepherd and his sheep, the theme of judgement is still prominent.

First, Jesus distinguishes between two kinds of people who go into sheepfolds—there are those who use the door put there for the purpose and those who choose some other way in. The shepherd is known to the gatekeeper and to the sheep. Because of the shepherd's personal knowledge of the sheep they are willing to follow him wherever he leads. They would do the opposite for strangers. This allegorical parable is lost upon the Pharisees. They are unable to apply the teaching of Ezek. 34 about the true and false shepherds of Israel to their own situation.

Jesus therefore has to be more explicit. He identifies Himself first of all with the door and then with the shepherd in two further 'I am' sayings. Other claimants to spiritual authority over the people of God had a destructive purpose in coming. The purpose of His coming was to bring life—life in far fuller measure than they had ever had it before.

For the people listening to Christ, the picture of a shepherd calling his sheep one by one, by name, was familiar (3,27). It is a vivid picture of the fact that God knows people as individuals. In 1929 Dr. L.P. Jacks wrote a prayer which ended 'Help us to regard each son of man not by his number but by his name'. Since then, vast increases in the population have made the impersonal numbering of people and the placing of them under tighter control, almost inevitable. But God has not changed, He still knows His people by name—an indication of His loving care for us as individuals.

Notes: V. 1: 'the sheepfold' was probably the enclosed courtyard of a house. Some have seen significance in the description of Judas as a 'thief' (**12.**6) and Barabbas as a 'robber' (**18.**40), but it is false spiritual claimants who are in view in the first instance. V. 4: 'brought out' comes from the same word as 'cast out' in **9.**34. It may suggest His bringing His flock out of the fold of Judaism. V. 6: 'figure'. This is not the same as the sort of parable usually found in the Synoptic Gospels. It means a symbolic utterance but not every detail is necessarily symbolic. V. 9: here as in v. 7 a second metaphor is introduced, comparing Jesus to the door as well as to the shepherd. This 'I am' saying is similar to that recorded in **14.**6. Access to God is through Christ alone.

St. John 10.11-21

Now we come to the specific identification of Jesus with the shepherd. The proof that He is the good Shepherd is shown not by any outward office or external display of strength but by the fact of His sacrificial love for the sheep. There is a clear contrast between Him and those whose supposed work of shepherding is done not for love but for financial or other reward. When it comes to the crunch, they do not really care about the sheep. Jesus, on the other hand, has such a knowledge of His sheep and such a love for them, that He is prepared to lay down His life for them. Not all His sheep are to be found within the fold of Palestinian Judaism. He will unite His flock which is at present scattered all over the world.

The secret of all this is not that Jesus will accept a martyr's death which He cannot avoid. It is rather that He lays His life down voluntarily and with a specific purpose. He lays it down in order to take it up again. This is a fulfilment of His Father's command and a reason for His Father's love. Once again His claims bring division and a charge of demon-possession and madness (cf. **7**.43; **9**.16). Once again a gap opens between those who have written Him off and those who will consider the evidence.

Notes: V. 11: 'good'—the particular word used here (*kalos*) suggests a moral beauty and attractiveness. This is shown to every generation in His love to the death for us. The figure of the shepherd was applied frequently to God in the O.T. and also to such leaders of Israel as Moses and David. It is not by itself necessarily a Messianic title. V. 12: 'wolf'—there is no need to try to identify this precisely. The point at issue is the different attitude of the true and false shepherds. The point, so far as Christian ministry is concerned, is well made in 1 Pet. **5**.2–4. Vs. 14 f.: the relationship between Christ and the believer is derived from the relationship between the Father and the Son (cf. **15**.9; **17**.21; **20**.21). V. 16: 'one flock'—the AV (KJV) translation 'one fold' could be seriously misleading. The people of God is one, even if denominational and other differences exist. The 'other sheep' may in the first instance be the Jews of the Dispersion but the thought of the Gentiles lies in the background.

St. John 10.22-30

The visit of Jesus to the Feast of Tabernacles, which has occupied a large section of the Book of Signs (**7**.10—**10**.21), has ended in division. This is the inevitable effect of light coming into the world (**3**.19–21). After a further two or three months, He comes back to Jerusalem to make His last challenge before the final crisis. The festival in question was the Feast of Dedication (or *Hanukkah*). The Temple, which had been desecrated by Antiochus Epiphanes in 168 B.C., was rededicated by Judas Maccabaeus three years later and this was commemorated annually in late December. (It is of course possible that the visit to the Feast of Tabernacles ended earlier, and that to the Feast of Dedication began earlier, perhaps at the beginning of ch. **9**.)

It seems that Jesus did not take the initiative in pressing His claims but was available to be questioned further about them. The uncertainty and speculation had evidently not abated and He is now pressed to make an unequivocal statement as to whether or not He is the Christ. But an apparently straight answer would be misleading in view of the climate of belief and Jesus points them yet again to His deeds as the evidence (cf. **5**.36; **10**.37 f.; **14**.11).

What is wrong is not the evidence but the fact that they do not belong to Him. If they belonged to His sheep their obedience and discipleship would be evident and there would never be any doubt about their salvation. The unity of Father and Son meant that if they enjoyed the protection of the Son, they enjoyed the protection of the Father also.

Notes: V. 23: 'winter'—as this was always a winter festival perhaps this is an eyewitness touch which is meant to emphasize the particularly cold weather. The reference to the portico and to the Jews gathering round in a circle seem to be similar touches. Vs. 26–28: the fault of unbelief is in them and not in Him. There is in this passage as strong a strain of predestination as there is in the Pauline epistles. The positive side of it provides the only foundation for the Christian life. V. 30: the oneness is more than just of will. But the two Persons are still distinguished.

St. John 10.31-42

This last assertion of Jesus is such that for the second time the desire of the Jews to kill Him actually got as far as their picking up stones to throw at Him (cf. **8**.59; **11**.8). Jesus again reminds them of the evidence of His deeds. For which of them does He deserve to be stoned? For none of them, they tell Him, but for blasphemy. The charge of blasphemy is put in its most succinct form—'You, being a man, make Yourself God'. Here is one of the great ironies of the Gospel. The one who was 'God' (**1**.1) had become man (**1**.14) in an amazing act of loving condescension. Such is their failure in perspective through their moral blindness that they see everything the wrong way round.

Jesus answers their objections with a piece of rabbinic argument. If they look at the Scriptures they will see that the name 'gods' could be applied to the judges of Israel because they were exercising a divinely appointed function. They accept the authority of the

Scriptures which allow such a title. Why then object to the application of the title 'Son of God' to one sent by the Father? The proof of it all is again His deeds. Their attitude to His words was of less importance than what they made of the evidence before their eyes. Again argument gives way to an abortive attempt at arrest (cf. 7.30,44; **8.**20).

Jesus then retired briefly before the final conflict. Many people came to see Him there and on meeting Him confirmed that John, though no miracle-worker, had achieved his purpose in giving faithful evidence about Jesus. So they believed in Him (cf. **1.**6–8). 'Where the preaching of repentance has had success, there the preaching of reconciliation and gospel grace is most likely to be prosperous. Where John has been acceptable, Jesus will not be unacceptable' (M. Henry). ·

Notes: V. 34: this would be a most unusual argument for any Christian to invent, because it does not distinguish Christ from other men clearly enough. He argues with them on their own terms. V. 36: 'consecrated'. He in His own person fulfils the Feast of Dedication. This consecration will reach its climax in His death (**17.**19). V. 42: their faith must still be imperfect as He has not yet fully revealed Himself through His death and resurrection.

Meditation: 'John did no sign, but everything that John said about this man was true' (41). The secret of spiritual success is not in the spectacular but in a consistent witness to Jesus Christ. Have we the humility to accept this role for ourselves?

St. John 11.1-16

The stage is now set for the greatest of all Jesus' signs other than the resurrection itself. He has shown mastery over the natural order and over disease. If death had previously had a potential victim snatched from its jaws (**4.**46–54), now it must yield up a man who has been in its domain for four days. Here is the Prince of life in action as He goes to His death.

The last sign, like the first, takes place within a family circle and is specifically said to show the glory of God and of Christ (**2.**11; **11.**4,40). Despite the urgent call of Mary and Martha and His special affection for the family, Jesus delayed visiting the sick Lazarus, for He saw the divine purpose in the whole incident. Eventually He told His disciples that He was going to Judea again. Despite the protests of the disciples about the dangers facing them in Judea, He insists that His work must be done at the right time.

49

As they misunderstand His allusions He has to tell them outright that Lazarus has died and that the purpose of their visit was to raise him. Thomas sees only death ahead and urges his fellow-disciples to come and face it with Jesus.

Notes: The historical character of this story has been more questioned than that of any other in the Gospel. The real problem is not whether Jesus could raise the dead (that was part of the Messianic claim—Luke 7.11–17,22) but why such a vivid demonstration of this power, which had such important consequences, was not recorded in the other Gospels. It must be said that the vivid detail speaks strongly for the story's being factual. The simplest possible reason for its not being mentioned in *Mark* is that Peter was not present, but that is merely speculation. V. 1: Lazarus and his sisters are the only persons named in a miracle story in the Gospel apart from members of the Twelve. Lazarus means 'God helps'. Mary and Martha are mentioned in Luke 10.38–42, and the name Lazarus is used in a parable in Luke 16.19–31. V. 4: 'not unto death'—death would not be the end of it. As an opportunity of glorifying God, cf. 9.3. Every affliction is an opportunity. Vs. 5 f.: the reason for His delay is surprisingly His love for the family. His absence will be the means of their faith (15). V. 16: Thomas is quite prominent in the latter chapters of the Gospel as a man of action slightly bewildered by the events around him (14.5; 20.24,26,29; 21.2).

St. John 11.17-27

Jesus arrives on the scene, not only too late to save Lazarus from dying, but also to find him already buried for four days. Many people from Jerusalem have come to console the sisters. The news then comes that Jesus is on the way. It is Martha, the active and aggressive sister, who goes out to meet Him and apparently rebukes Him for His slowness in coming. She and her sister do not have faith like that of the centurion, that a word spoken from a distance would suffice. They expected Jesus to come back with their messenger, and the fact that He did not do so must have seemed to them hard and inexplicable. Even so Martha's faith in Him remains and she knows that He will be able to do something to help.

Jesus tells Martha that her brother will rise again. This is taken by her as merely an orthodox statement of belief. She knows that he will in the end. Jesus then speaks to her the fifth of the 'I am' sayings. He is the resurrection and the life—faith in Him means in one way the overcoming of death and in another the avoiding of it.

50

When He asks whether she believes this, her reply is a confession of faith in Him as Christ and Son of God without any reference to His claim to raise the dead.

Martha and Mary both say the same—'if you had been here . . .' But if He had, their faith would not have been tested, and neither they nor the other people with them would have seen the great sign of eternal life. God delays for a purpose, and this is surely an encouragement to us in those trying times when His failure to intervene seems to us both endless and purposeless.

Notes: V. 17: he would have been buried on the day he died. V. 18: this fact may be recorded in order to show that He was not far away from a still greater raising of the dead from which alone all other signs drew their significance. V. 19: there would be seven days of solemn mourning. 'The Jews' are representative of the Judeans who are about to be given their last chance to believe. V. 21: even if there may be a note of reproach, it is more in sorrow than in anger, and her faith in Him remains. Vs. 25 f.: the relationship of physical and spiritual life and death has already been foreshadowed in **5.**25–29. Here was the proof that the hour was not only coming but had actually arrived. Martha's orthodox faith had to be turned into a living experience through seeing Christ in action. So has ours today.

St. John 11.28-37

Martha may at times have been a difficult person to live with (Luke **10.**40), but she had a sense of responsibility. She went to Mary, and aware of her sensitive nature she called her quietly, saying that Jesus had specifically asked for her. She too had to be involved in the amazing event that was to happen. Mary went off, not, as the Jews supposed, to weep hopelessly for her dead brother, but to meet the Lord of life. Her words to Jesus are the same as Martha's. They both believed that He could have prevented the tragedy, and fail to understand why it was that He had not come when they had called for Him.

Jesus is deeply affected by the sight of mourning which confronts Him. When they take Him to the tomb, He too weeps. To the Jews this is evidence of His love for Lazarus and some of them too wonder why He did not intervene sooner. But it seems that Jesus' weeping goes a good deal deeper than sympathy. There is an anger about it. This is probably, at the deepest level, anger against sin and death and the terrible hold which they have on the human race. Perhaps there was also anger at the unbelief or half-belief of

51

those who could not see that He was able to fulfil His claims to raise the dead. His weeping, in any event, is not on the same level as theirs. It is His preparation for grappling with the power of death here and on the cross (Heb. **2**.14 f.; cf. Heb. **5**.7–9).

Notes: V. 28: 'The Teacher' may have been the name by which He was known to the family. It is an inadequate description of Him at this crisis. V. 32: Mary's action is more impetuous than Martha's. Jesus does not try to explain things to her but goes straight into action. V. 33: for His being troubled as He faced His passion, cf. **12**.27; **13**.21. Our redemption was achieved at tremendous cost to Him. V. 34: the only occasion in the Gospel on which He asks for information. V. 36: it was not His weeping but His death which was to show His love, not only for Lazarus, but for the whole world.

St. John 11.38-44

Jesus is inwardly stirred again as He prepares to wrestle with sin and death. He gives the simple order that the stone should be removed: Martha keeps her feet firmly on the ground. This is an impossible command. A putrefying body will give off an appalling stench after four days in a warm climate. Only the firm assurance of Jesus that faith is necessary and the glory of God is the object, causes them to obey.

Jesus then addresses a prayer to His Father, acknowledging His dependence in this particular action and thanking Him that He has already heard. He adds words which emphasize His confidence that His Father always hears His prayers. He has said what He has in order that the crowd should see this, not as a display of wonder-working, but as the most impressive of His signs to show that He was sent by God to do God's work.

Action has been taken, prayer has been offered, now comes the word of life. There is no mystical formula but a straightforward command (cf. **5**.8; Mark **5**.41). So the dead hears the voice of the Son of God and hearing lives and comes forth from his tomb (**5**.25–29). The trappings of death are still all over him. Jesus tells them to untie them and release him. The liberation He brings is meant to be complete.

Notes: V. 39: 'Take away the stone'—this and the unwinding of the graveclothes needed human co-operation. In His own resurrection no human agency was involved (**20**.1–10). Further than that, of course, Lazarus had his natural body restored to him and, though we hear no more of him, after **12**.10, in due course died again, Jesus was raised in His spiritual body, the mortal put on immortality (1 Cor. **15**.54). Vs. 41 f.: apart from the long prayer of ch. **17,** there is only one other occasion in the Gospel when Jesus is clearly recorded as addressing His Father (**12**.27 f.). However, it is quite probable that His words from the cross (**19**.28–30) were spoken primarily to His Father and not to men.

St. John 11.45-57

Surely this supreme and incontrovertible demonstration of Jesus' power will lead to His acceptance by those who have seen it and those who hear their evidence! Many who had come with Mary believed. But others, no doubt still bewildered, went to tell the Pharisees. They joined together with the chief priests to call a council. They do not now deny that Jesus is doing signs. The evidence is too strong for that. Nor, however, will they accept what the facts are shrieking at them, that this man is acting with the power of God, for He has been sent by God (cf. Mark **3**.22).

There is no attempt now at theological assessment. They have already made up their minds and they are confirmed in their resolution now that such an obvious threat to their position is developing. There is such a danger of a popular uprising that it will lead to counter-action by the Romans and that will be the end of both Temple and nation. It is the high priest, of all people, who with cynical expediency chooses the victim for sacrifice. In this master-piece of dramatic irony he decides that one man should die that the people should live. He spoke far more than he could ever know, for that was the purpose of Jesus' mission, which stretched far beyond the confines of Palestine to all God's scattered children (**3**.16). Now the issue is settled and they will pursue Him relentlessly to death.

The statement of Caiaphas, and the decision and subsequent action of the Council, illustrate what is frequently stated in Scripture—that God can take the evil that men do and weave it into a larger pattern which is for His glory and the good of other people. Caiaphas acted as a free agent, personally responsible for what he did. God, however, used his action without destroying his freedom, and turned evil into glory.

Jesus knew the situation clearly enough and withdrew to Ephraim. When the Passover came there was widespread speculation as to whether He would come to Jerusalem or not.

Notes: V. 47: the chief priests, who were Sadducees, were thrown into alliance with their rivals the Pharisees through common opposition to Jesus. The priests now take the leading role and the

53

Pharisees are only mentioned in **12.**19,42. V. 48: ironically this is just what the Romans did do in A.D. 70. They thought of '*our* holy place' as if it belonged to them, not God (cf. Matt. **23.**38). But Jesus made a new temple (**2.**19–22) and gathers the people of God on a new basis (**3.**16; **10.**16). V. 49: the high priest was unwittingly exercising his power of prophecy, despite his arrogant claim to knowledge (cf. **7.**47–49; 1 Cor. **2.**8). The office did not change annually—he was high priest that memorable year.

To think over: '**You** *meant evil . . . but God meant . . . good*' *(Gen.* **50.***20).*

Questions for further study and discussion on St. John chs. 10 and 11
1. What principles of pastoral care may be found in **10.**1–18?
2. What effect should the knowledge of belonging to Christ's sheep have on us (**10.**25–30)?
3. Can illness and a delay in answer to prayer still be to God's glory (**11.**1–6)?
4. How far has the living experience of Christ, the resurrection and the life (**11.**25 f.), transformed our attitude to life and to death?
5. When did we last let our vested interest in the religious *status quo* dull our response to new truth (**11.**45–53)?

St. John 12.1-11

Now there begin the momentous events of the last week of the ministry of Jesus. While the ordinary people are divided and the Roman authorities have not yet been asked to show their hand, the Jewish leaders are inexorably committed to getting rid of Him and well aware that they must take action at the time of the Passover festival.

Jesus still goes calmly on His way and enjoys a meal with Lazarus and his sisters. The domesticated Martha sees to the arrangements while Mary, in an act of extravagant devotion, anoints His feet with expensive ointment and wipes them with her hair. Sensitive people, whose capacity for grief and sorrow is great, have the compensation that they can also rise to great heights of love and devotion. Judas fails to see the point of such seeming waste. Far better use the money for charity, though his idea of charity seemed to be concerned more with himself than with the poor. But Mary had kept the ointment for this significant and unrepeatable moment, in preparation for the burial of Jesus. There would be many further opportunities of helping the poor, many of them inspired in fact by His death for mankind.

News soon got round that Jesus was after all in the vicinity, so the crowds turned out to see Him. They were also interested in seeing the unusual phenomenon of a dead man who had come to life again. This living evidence of the truth of His claims was winning supporters for Jesus, so the chief priests decided that he too must be got rid of.

Notes: V. 1: the raising of Lazarus is emphasized again, as being a major cause of the crucifixion. V. 3: the story relates the same event as that recorded in Mark **14.**3–9, but a different one from that in Luke **7.**36–38. V. 6: it looks as if Judas had been made treasurer of the band because of financial ability, but his strength was also his weakness. V. 7: a very difficult construction. Most probably it means: 'Let her alone (she has not sold it for the poor) that she may keep it for the day of My burial' (which she was here anticipating). V. 10: a natural reaction from Sadducees to remove a man whose very presence refuted their disbelief in resurrection (Mark **12.**18).

A point to ponder: If, as we have suggested, temptation frequently comes to us along the lines of our greatest gifts and sin is often the perversion of our ability, how can we ensure that God is in complete control of all our abilities?

St. John 12.12-19

A great crowd of the Jews had come out to Bethany to see Jesus and Lazarus. Now a great crowd of those who had come as pilgrims to the festival hear that Jesus is coming to Jerusalem and set out to meet Him. They took with them branches of palm trees such as had been used to hail Simon Maccabaeus after his victory (1 Macc. **13.**51). They greeted Him with words from Psa. **118,** which was in use at the Passover, applying the words to Him as the King of Israel. There is no doubt that they were giving Him a Messianic welcome into the city. He could not now avoid being King as He had done before in Galilee (**6.**15).

But Jesus will not have Messiahship of the sort that they are looking for. He must come into Jerusalem but He does so, not on a regal charger, but on an ass, the beast of burden symbolizing peace. His interpretation of the incident was based on Zech. **9.**9 and was more far-reaching than theirs. For the passage was in a context of the Messiah's universal reign of peace and His liberating mission through the blood of the covenant. No wonder the disciples did not understand this until after the resurrection (cf. **2.**22; **14.**26). The excitement of Messianic expectation had spread from crowd to crowd until it seemed to the despairing Pharisees that the whole

world had gone after Him. They, like the high priest, were pro-
phesying unwittingly.

Notes: The story occurs in all four Gospels. There are some
minor differences between the account in John and the others.
V. 13: 'Hosanna'—a Hebrew word meaning 'save now'. It had the
general force of 'Hail!' V. 15: this is a free rendering of Zech. **9**.9.
'Fear not' could be an echo of Isa. **40**.9.

St. John 12.20-26

The world seems to have gone after Him in the Pharisees' eyes.
And so it is because some of the pilgrims at the festival were Greeks.
Whether these were Gentile proselytes or Greek-speaking Jews is
not certain. What is important is that the mission of Jesus is shown
to extend beyond the confines of Palestinian Judaism. And it is a
Galilean with a Greek name—Philip—whom they approach with
their request to see Jesus. The Judeans had had their chance to
see Him during His ministry, and these pilgrims seem to want the
same privilege. He is soon to hide Himself finally (36).

We are not told whether their request was granted. But Jesus sees
it as an extremely significant occasion. Now was the hour of
glorification. And glory was to come to the Son of man through
death. It was only in death that there lay the possibility of growth.
It was only in the death of one Man for the people that there lay
the hope of the salvation of the whole world. What applies to the
mission of Jesus applies also to the mission of His disciples. The
willingness to lose our lives in the cause of Christ is the only true
way of serving Him. Nevertheless, we still find His teaching hard to
understand and harder still to follow. Almost everything in 'this
world' conditions us to think that the man who 'loses his life in this
world' has lost it. We need to remind ourselves of the grain of
wheat—the simple, true fact of everyday life, which is also a most
profound truth of spiritual life.

Notes: V. 20: it is unlikely that these were Gentile 'Godfearers'
as they would probably not come up to Jerusalem for the festivals.
The principles of the Gentile mission are firmly laid in the Gospel
even if the Romans may be the only Gentiles with whom Jesus
comes in contact. V. 23: 'the Greeks' may be included in this as
well as Philip and Andrew. 'Glorified': this term covered the whole
redemptive action which Jesus was about to perform. In the divine
paradox the cross was no less glorious than any other part of His
work. V. 25: the paradox of redemption applies also to discipleship. Only in its death does the self discover what it is meant to be.

For meditation: 'To serve Jesus is to follow Him, and He is going to death' (26, Barrett).

St. John 12.27-36

As Jesus enters into the supreme crisis, not only in His own ministry but in the history of the world, He cries out to His Father for strength and guidance. However tempting it might be to try to avoid the horrors that lay ahead of Him, He will not do it. He knows it is His hour at last. He knows that the purpose of it all is to glorify His Father's name. It is for that that He asks, and a heavenly voice assures Him that His prayer has been and will be answered. As usual the bystanders misunderstand. They no more grasp the meaning of the heavenly voice than they have done the meaning of the words of Jesus.

If this had seemed a strange time to be speaking of glory, it is an equally unusual one to refer to judgement when it is not judgement of Jesus but judgement of the world and the devil which is meant. But paradox cannot be avoided and it is His exaltation in death that will be the means of life for all.

Still people do not understand. Still they do not know who this mysterious Son of man is. So Jesus can only give them an urgent exhortation concerning the need to act while the light is there with them in His person. Faith in Him will change their whole being. And with that final challenge He goes, hidden from them until He appears as a prisoner about to be put to death.

Notes: V. 27: John does not describe the agony in the Garden of Gethsemane. This passage shows that he is aware of the real moral struggle which Jesus had to undergo as He faced death for the sins of the world. V. 28: the nature of the heavenly voice is not clear. The crowd heard the sound without distinguishing the words (cf. Acts **9**.7; **22**.9). V. 31: for the cross as a victory over the devil, cf. Col. **2**.15. V. 32: the idea of being 'lifted up' was important because of its double meaning (cf. **8**.28; Gen. **40**.20) and also because it specified death by crucifixion rather than by stoning or in any other way. V. 34: the passages in the Law referred to possibly include Psa. **89**.4,29,36; Isa. **9**.7; Ezek. **37**.25.

St. John 12.37-43

We are now coming to the end of the 'Book of Signs' and the evangelist gives us a brief summary of the lack of success of Jesus' mission and the reasons for that. Signs were meant to be an aid to faith so that men should have life. That is why the evangelist himself took the trouble to write them down (**20**.31). But for the majority of the people the signs did not have this effect. All sorts of excuses were made at various stages of the Gospel why men should not believe in Jesus. It was possible to question the evidence in one way or another, or to form *a priori* theological opinions that Jesus could not be a man of God, or simply to crush the suggestion from a position of ecclesiastical privilege.

But it would be wrong to look for the whole cause merely at the human level. The trouble went deeper than that. For this was a fulfilment of prophecy. In Isa. **53**.1 the fact of unbelief had been stated, and when the suffering servant of the Lord came, that had to be fulfilled. In Isa. **6**.10 the prophet went further and attributed unbelief to the action of God who blinded them.

Despite all this, there was not a clear-cut rejection of Jesus' claims. There were many secret believers who were anxious not to lose their position in Judaism, especially those of them who were among the authorities. They come under the devastating condemnation that they preferred to be praised by men than by God.

Notes: This brief review of the ministry by the evangelist is similar to the writer's assessment of the history of the northern kingdom of Israel in 2 Kings **17**. V. 40: the apparent failure of the mission of Jesus was accounted for in the Synoptic Gospels also by the quotation from Isa. **6**.10 (cf. Mark **4**.11 f.; **8**.17 f.; also Acts **28**.26 f.). The sense of the fulfilment of the divine purpose is supposed to complement rather than override human moral responsibility (cf. Acts **2**.23). V. 43: Nicodemus and Joseph became bolder later (**19**.38–42). Perhaps someone like Gamaliel was also a secret believer (Acts **5**.34–39).

St. John 12.44-50

'The Book of Signs' finally closes with a summary of Jesus' message, as if in a final presentation of it to an unbelieving or half-believing Judaism. Here we have, in concentrated form, themes which have been dealt with at greater length previously. Here there is faith and sight, the Son as the representative of the Father, light, judgement, authority and life.

For this reading it would be well to 're-cap' over 'The Book of Signs' and see the way in which these themes have been developed previously.

Vs.44f. Believing in and seeing Jesus is the equivalent of believing in and seeing God: cf. **1**.14–18; **6**.27–29,35–40,44–47. (Look forward also to **14**.1–11.) It is not necessary to establish the fact of God's existence before beginning to talk about Christ. We can begin the other way round—with the Man, Jesus, with His life, His words and His actions. 'God is Christlike and in Him is no unChristlikeness at all' (Ramsey). This is why history is of such importance and Christian truth is unique. It is the truth that in the man Jesus, God Himself was known, seen and heard.

V.46. Jesus is the light of the world, and those who believe in Him are delivered from darkness: cf. **1**.4–9; **3**.21; **8**.12; **9**.4 f.; **11**.9; **12**.35 f.

Vs. 47 f. Jesus did not come to judge the world but to save the world: cf. **3**.14–18; **8**.15; **10**.9 f. Nevertheless His word will judge those who reject Him and do not keep His sayings: cf. **3**.19 f., 34–36; **5**.19–30,45–47; **8**.26,31–51; **9**.39–41. (Look forward also to **14**.23 f.)

Vs. 49 f. Jesus' words have been spoken not on His own authority but according to His Father's command: cf. **3**.31–35; **5**.19 f., 30–37; **7**.16–18; **8**.26–29,39–47. (Look forward also to **14**.10.) The Son's word, spoken according to the Father's command, gives life: cf. **1**.4; **3**.16 f., 36; **4**.46–54; **5**.24–29; **6**.35–40,47–58,63,68 f.; **10**.10,27 f.; **11**.25 f., 43 f.; **12**.25. (Look forward also to **14**.6,19; **17**.2 f.; **20**.31.)

In view of the reference to Jesus' hiding Himself in **12**.36, there seems little doubt that this section was not supposed to have been spoken by Jesus at this time, but that it is a summary of His words by the evangelist in the way that vs. 37–43 are a summary of the response to His works.

Questions for further study and discussion on St. John ch. 12
1. How should we aim to achieve a balance between time and money spent on worship and on charity (**12**.1–8)?
2. Do people ask us to help them to see Jesus (**12**.21)? If not, why not? If so, can we help them effectively?
3. How has Jesus' statement in **12**.31 f. been fulfilled in the history of the Church?
4. What do the principles of life through death (**12**.24–26) mean in practice in your life?
5. What is our attitude to the light (**12**.35 f.)?

St. John 13.1-11

So far Jesus has been putting His claims, by deed and word, before the people of God, whose response has been largely negative. Now the last appeal has been made to the Jews. The rest of the Gospel has been called 'The Book of the Passion'. The great sign is that of His death and resurrection. This is preceded by the discourses which explain it and its consequences. The teaching is now no longer given openly to the world but privately to His disciples.

The Feast of the Passover gives us the theological setting for what follows. The festival which commemorated the great act of redemption of the Old Covenant was to be the setting of the great act of redemption of the New. The hour, which Jesus or the evangelist had referred to earlier as not yet having arrived (**2.4**; **7.30**; **8.**20), has now come (**12.**23). Jesus must return via death to the Father. His mind was fully assured of His divine origin and destination. The necessary work of the traitor, inspired by the devil, was already in hand. In this context, where so many other emotions may have been present, His dominant characteristic is love. This is shown in a demonstration of humble service towards His disciples.

The foot-washing also had a symbolic meaning. Peter at first impetuously refuses to be washed and then asks to be washed all over! But Jesus explains that when a man has once been made clean all over, then this is all that is necessary afterwards. All His disciples apart from Judas had been made clean.

Notes: V. 1: NEB: 'now He was to show the full extent of His love'—not only in the foot-washing, but in the cross. V. 2: for the devil and Judas, see **6.**70 f.; **13.**27. 'His own' are now the disciples rather than the Jews (**1.**11), but it is the member of the Twelve, who was probably the only Judean and who bore the very name of Judah, who was to betray Him. V. 4: 'laid aside'—the same word as is used for laying down His life (**10.**11,15,17 f.). V. 7: the Spirit would enlighten them and show them that they needed to accept service from Christ before they could serve. V. 10: there is a once-for-all cleansing, symbolized by baptism and dependent upon the 'baptism' of Christ in His death (Mark **10.**38; Luke **12.**50). There is also the need for daily cleansing and forgiveness. Some MSS, however, omit 'except for his feet'.

St. John 13.12-20

Jesus now takes His clothes again and resumes His place. The whole action suggests that it is, amongst other things, a vivid demonstration of His death, resurrection and exaltation. He laid aside His clothes as He lays down His life (**10.**11,15,17 f.). He takes His clothes as He takes His life again (**10.**17 f.), and He resumes His place as He returns to His Father (**6.**62; **13.**1). The pattern is such as is described in Paul's great 'Christological hymn' (Phil. **2.**5–11).

It is not, however, the theological movement which He wishes to make explicit at this juncture. It is rather the moral and social consequences. They rightly put Him in a place of authority and yet He had done a menial service for them. How much more then should they be willing to serve one another! There is not much in any of the Gospels which is specifically referred to as 'an example', therefore all the more importance must be attached to this. Blessedness was promised to those who knew this—but on one important condition—that they did it. Jesus reaffirms that He knows that not everyone even of the Twelve will do this. The Scripture had to be fulfilled concerning the traitor, and His foreknowledge of this fact should help them to understand that He was the Messiah. Receiving them was receiving Him, and was also receiving the Father.

Notes: V. 13: Jesus is elsewhere called 'Teacher' in **11**.28 and 'Rabbi' in **1**.38,49; **3**.2; **20**.16. The idea of Him as 'Lord' is a prominent one in the Gospel and comes especially frequently in chs. **13** and **14**. Rabbis could expect some acts of menial service from their disciples, and masters could demand them from their slaves. Here the roles are strikingly reversed. V. 16: 'he who is sent' —the Greek word *apostolos* (apostle) is used here only in the Gospel and in a non-technical sense. V. 18: 'lifted his heel'—this either pictures a horse kicking back at a man or someone shaking the dust off his feet. V. 19: 'I am He'—cf. **8**.24. V. 20: this is what gives the work of the disciples such significance (cf. Matt. **10**.40). Their mission from Him is similar to His from the Father (**20**.21). For reaction to the Son being reaction to the Father, see **5**.23; **8**.19; **12**.44 f.; **14**.7,9; **15**.23.

For meditation: The call to service (14 ff.) is based on the fact that Christ first serves us, even to the point of dying for us. 'Every disciple and every company of disciples need to learn that their first duty is to let Christ serve them' (Temple).

St. John 13.21-30

There have been a number of allusions in this chapter to the traitor. Now Jesus, in distress of spirit, confronts the disciples openly with this fact. He solemnly asserts that one of them would betray Him. 'One of us? Surely not! Who on earth could it be?' Peter is determined to find out, so he asks the beloved disciple to ask Jesus. Because of his position of closeness to the Lord (literally 'in His bosom'—cf. **1**.18) he is able to ask Him. Jesus tells him that it is the person to whom He will give a morsel of bread. So Jesus hands it to Judas. As such an action showed that the recipient was an honoured guest, this was in effect a last appeal to Judas as well as an indication to John of the identity of the traitor.

If there had been any chance of a change of heart from Judas, it now disappears. Satan takes possession of him. So Jesus bids him do his deed quickly, as the agony of the last struggle comes increasingly upon Him. Apparently Judas was not suspected by the others, who simply thought Jesus was sending him on an errand. In an action full of tragic symbolism Judas went out from the room, from the circle of the disciples, from the presence of the Saviour of the world (cf. 1 John 2.18 f.). No wonder, as he turned his back on the Light of the world, it was night! (cf. 3.19). Divine love could go no further. Pursued to the very end by the love of Christ and yet still free to choose, Judas is typical of every man.

Notes: V. 21: while John does not record the agony in the Garden of Gethsemane, he emphasizes as much as the other evangelists the tremendous pressure there was upon Jesus as He prepared Himself to bear the sin of the world. V. 23: we assume that 'the beloved disciple', named here for the first time, is John. (See Introduction.) V. 26: it seems likely that Judas occupied the place of honour on the left of Jesus and that is why He was able to give him the morsel. This is, however, by no means sure. V. 29: this does not necessarily mean that the Passover had not begun, for the feast lasted for seven days.

St. John 13.31-38

When the Greeks had asked to see Him, Jesus had said, 'The hour has come for the Son of man to be glorified' (12.23), and His soul had been troubled as He considered what the 'hour' would mean (12.27). At the supper He is troubled again (21) as He contemplates the betrayal, and when the traitor has gone out into the night He repeats in similar terms, 'Now is the Son of man glorified' (31). Each step that brings death nearer brings glory nearer also, for there is glory even in His death. What is glory for the Son of man is glory also for God, for it is the final result of perfect obedience to His will.

Jesus now speaks, as He will do frequently in this discourse, of the fact that He must leave the disciples very soon and go to a sphere of existence which they will not be able to penetrate. If He is to be absent in body His presence may still be known in their midst. It will be demonstrated clearly to all men by the new Christian virtue of love. This was a love that was to spring out of His love for them (13.1,15,35).

Peter inevitably wishes to know where Jesus is going and to follow Him even if it means laying down his life. Fine words and sincerely meant. But he does not know what lies ahead and, Jesus, with sounder knowledge of coming events and of human nature, has to tell him sadly that he will deny Him three times before morning.

Notes: V. 33: 'little children'—this is the only time this word is used in the Gospel, though it is used seven times in *1 John*. A similar word is found in **21**.5. 'A little while'—cf. **14**.19; **16**.16–19. 'As I said to the Jews'—see **7**.33 f.; **8**.21. V. 34: 'a new commandment'. This was not new in the sense that it had never been commanded previously, for the Law had told them to love their neighbours as themselves (Lev. **19**.18). It was new in the sense that the love of God had been demonstrated by the sending of His Son (**3**.16) who had Himself loved them right to the end (**13**.1). Their mutual love was to be a reflection of that, which gave it a new dynamic. V. 38: Peter's failure to submit patiently to Christ and obey Him, shown already in his attitude to the foot-washing, will have shameful consequences. So does ours!

St. John 14.1-7

In the face of the disturbed atmosphere among the disciples—His saying that He will leave them and His prediction of Peter's denial—Jesus tells them not to be troubled. Such a situation was an occasion for faith in the Father and the Son. There were many places in heaven. His departure was in order to make them ready for His disciples. Nor did He intend to leave them for ever, for He would return and take them to Himself so that their fellowship might be restored and continue.

When Jesus asserts that they know the way where He is going, Thomas protests that as they do not know the destination they cannot possibly know the route. This gives Jesus the chance to deliver another of the 'I am' sayings. He Himself is the way, the truth and the life. Because He is the truth and the life, He is the exclusive way to the Father. No one can reach the Father except through Him. The bewilderment about the Father was due to their state of muddle about who Jesus was. To know Him as what He really was would be to know the Father too (**8**.19).

Notes: V. 2: 'rooms'—the word means places to stop and remain in rather than progressive halts on a journey (cf. v. 23). The NEB renders as the AV (KJV): 'if it were not so I should have told you.' The difficulty with the RSV translation is that Jesus has not specifically been recorded as having told them that He was going to prepare a place for them. V. 3: 'I will come again'—the primary reference seems to be to the second coming or to His receiving each disciple at death. But the succeeding passages show a great emphasis on His coming through the resurrection and the Holy Spirit (**14**.18,28; **16**.16,22). V. 6: 'the way, the truth and the life'—in the context it is clear that the second and third words explain further what Jesus means by the first. He is the true way and the living way. 'Life' is a word which occurs with particular frequency in the first twelve chapters, 'truth' an almost equal number of times in chs. **1–12** and **13–21**.

St. John 14.8-14

Even at this stage of the ministry the disciples are still baffled about many of the leading themes of Jesus' teaching and they still fail to understand the nature of His relationship to the Father. If Jesus talks darkly about knowing and seeing the Father, Philip is not satisfied. Let us have a proper revelation of God (a 'theophany' such as Moses had had—Exod. **24**.10). We shall see Him with our own eyes. There will no longer be any doubt. We shall really be satisfied then.

Jesus sadly has to point out to Philip his failure to grasp who He is. The mutual indwelling of Father and Son was a basic thing which the disciples ought to have grasped. This was shown by His teaching which was not given simply on His own authority. It was also demonstrated by His miracles which were not the deeds of a mere man.

Having used His doing the works of God as evidence of His relationship to the Father, Jesus, no doubt to their great surprise, goes on to say that the disciples will do even greater deeds because of His return to the Father. The glorification of the Father in the Son was not to end with the earthly life of the Son. Through prayer it would be continued, and the scope of prayer is vast, limited only by the important condition that it should be in His name.

Notes: V: 8: Philip is mentioned on four occasions in the Gospel (**1**.43–48; **6**.5–7; **12**.20–22). He seems to have been enthusiastic but uncomprehending. V. 9: to see Jesus is to see the Father (cf. **12**.45). The same applies to honouring Him (**5**.23), knowing Him (**8**.19; **14**.7), believing in Him (**12**.44), receiving Him (**13**.20) and hating Him (**15**.23). This was due to their mutual indwelling. V. 12: 'greater works' because more far-reaching in their scope throughout the world and to all men. V. 13: 'in My name'—on My authority. It assumes obedience to His will, as He was obedient to the Father's will, and a true desire for the glorification of Father and Son. The promise has never been withdrawn and if it were taken seriously the effects would be incalculable.

Listening point : 'I cannot think what we shall find to do in heaven,' mused Luther. 'No work, no eating, no drinking, nothing to do. But I suppose there will be plenty to see.' 'Yes,' said Melancthon. '"Lord, show us the Father, and we shall be satisfied" (8).' 'Why, of course,' responded Luther, 'that sight will give us quite enough to do.'

St. John 14.15-24

Much of what Jesus says in the final discourse can only be understood in the light of the coming of the Holy Spirit. A new coming of the Spirit had been referred to by the evangelist in 7.39. Now Jesus devotes some time to explaining the personality of the Spirit, the nature of His coming and the work which He would do in the world.

The promise of the Spirit's coming is made in the context of the disciples' loving, and therefore obeying, their Master. The coming was to be in answer to the Son's prayer to the Father. The Spirit was described as the 'Counsellor'. He was to be there to stand by them and to help them. Despite the reality of the coming and the presence of the Spirit, the world at large would not recognize His presence or His existence. But the disciples would know from their experience.

Jesus now goes on to say that the Spirit's coming will be His own coming. As the days of His flesh come to an end the world will not be able to see Him any longer. His disciples, however, will go on seeing Him because His life will be in them through the Spirit. Only in the Spirit will they learn the mutual indwelling of Father and Son, and of themselves with Him. But this is not religious experience without moral consequences. Love and obedience are necessary for the continued enjoyment of the love of Father and Son, and for the reception of His revelation. There will be no fleeting visit. The man who loves and obeys will have the tremendous privilege of having Father and Son coming to make their home with Him through the Spirit.

Notes: V. 16: 'Counsellor'—the Greek word is *paraklētos*. It sometimes has the meaning of 'advocate' (so NEB). Christ is described as the believer's Paraclete or Advocate in 1 John 2.1. The Spirit is 'another' because He continues what Christ has done. There may be some connection also with the idea of Christian *paraklēsis* ('prophetic exhortation' to accept the Messianic sal-

vation; see Barrett's commentary ad loc.). V. 18: 'desolate'—
literally 'orphans'. The word was used of disciples who had lost a
teacher as well as of children who had lost a father.

St. John 14.25-31

Not only was the presence and power of Jesus limited in the incarnation, His teaching also had to be restricted. There were such obvious
limitations in the capacity of the disciples to understand. One of
the functions of the Holy Spirit was therefore to be that of teaching
them further and also reminding them of what Jesus had said. In
the new situation after the resurrection, with the new aid of the
Holy Spirit, they would be able to grasp His message and the meaning of His own person and mission in a new way. We too live in this
privileged position.

In the midst of so much that was disturbing, He promised them
peace. Not the superficial co-existence which the world allows at
times. This peace would reach through to the troubled heart. There
should be joy also from contemplation of the fact that He was
returning to the Father. The greatness of the Father meant the
exaltation of Christ and the fulfilment of the blessings which He
had promised would come to them through the Holy Spirit.

It was necessary for Jesus to let them know where He was going,
because they could easily have been confused (as in fact they were)
by the impending crisis. Satan was about to have his hour. He
had no power over Jesus. What was going to happen was done in
obedience to the Father's command and was a demonstration to
the world that He loved the Father.

Notes: V. 26: for the teaching function of the Spirit see also
15.26; **16.**13 f. For the disciples' understanding later what they
could not understand during the ministry see **2.**22; **12.**16; **13.**7.
V. 28: this does not imply any inferiority (see **10.**30). The Father is
the source and origin of everything and He is greater than the Son
in the sense that Jesus' mission was one of obedience to His Father's
will. It is a reference to the incarnate Jesus. V. 30: 'ruler of this
world', cf. **12.**31. Whatever the role of Satan, the fact remains that
in one sense Jesus' death was voluntary (**10.**18). V. 31: 'Rise, let us
go hence.' The presence of these words at this stage has caused a
number of scholars to suggest that chs. **15** and **16** should come
before this point. It may be, however, that the words should be
taken closely with the rest of the verse and are a moral exhortation
to go and meet the advancing enemy.

66

Questions for further study and discussion on St. John chs. 13 and 14

1. How far are we prepared to submit to Christ even when we do not understand (**13.**6–10)?
2. In what way can you follow the example which Christ gave in the foot-washing (**13.**14 f.)?
3. Why are the claims of Christ exclusive (**14.**6)?
4. Have we, in answer to prayer, experienced the power to do greater works than Jesus did (**14.**12 f.)? If not, why not?
5. Why is there such a close connection between love, obedience, and the presence of the Father and the Son (**14.**21–23)?

St. John 15.1-11

Mutual indwelling and mutual love have been the keynotes of ch. **14.** They are now strikingly illustrated by the figure of the vine and the branches, which provides the last of the 'I am' sayings and is further expounded in this chapter. Israel was frequently described in the O.T. as a vine (Psa. **80.**8; Jer. **2.**21; Hos. **10.**1) or as a vineyard (Isa. **5.**1–7). The metaphor suggests something belonging to God and tended by Him and expected in due course to yield fruit. This expectation was not fulfilled (Mark **12.**1–9). Israel, however, had only been a prefiguration of the Messiah, who was the true, genuine, real vine. Christ must not be thought of here simply as an individual, for by faith His people belong to Him and are united with Him. Consequently, He is the vine and they are the branches (5).

The main thrust of the figure now ceases to be the relationship of the vine to the vinedresser and becomes the relationship of the vine to the branches. The branches must be fruitful and become increasingly so. Fruit-bearing is only possible through the close union of vine and branches. When that occurs things will happen. The close union depends upon love and obedience. Fruitfulness brings glory to the Father and joy to the disciples, as we should discover for ourselves.

Notes: V. 1: the figure of the vine may have been suggested by the 'fruit of the vine' at the Last Supper (Mark **14.**25). V. 2: perhaps Judas and Peter are respectively in mind. V. 3: the disciples are in the position of having been pruned by the word of Jesus. V. 5: the metaphor is similar to the Pauline idea of 'in Christ' and his metaphor of 'the body of Christ' with its members. The fruit which is borne is first and foremost the fruit of Christian character (cf. Gal. **5.**22–24). V. 7: another striking promise about the efficacy of prayer but the basic conditions must not be forgotten (cf. **14.**13 f.). V. 8: it is important that there should be concrete evidence of their discipleship of Him (cf. **13**.35). V. 9: the relationship of Father to Son is repeated in the relationship of Christ to the disciples also in the sphere of mission (**20**.21). V. 11: 'My joy', cf. 'My peace' (**14**.27). For the fullness of joy, cf. **3**.29; **16**.24; **17**.13—see also Psa. **16**.11.

St. John 15.12-19

Once again we return to the all-important theme of love. The link between love for God and love for one's neighbour is so strong in John's Gospel that Kittel's 'Theological Word Book of the Bible' states: 'Love to God and Christ takes second place after love to the brethren.' There is some strong evidence for that rather surprising statement. But this love is no mere sentiment which can be worked up by a man at will or which comes irrationally upon him. Its source is the love of God shown in Christ and only those who have first meditated on, and responded to, that love are able to reflect it in their attitude to others. Jesus' love was proved by laying down His life. It was also proved by the way in which He treated His disciples as His friends, keeping them informed about what He was doing. His friendship to them was also shown by the fact that it was He who had chosen them, rather than the reverse.

If it was previously impossible to speak of light without mentioning darkness (**1**.4 f., etc.), now it is impossible to mention love without in the end coming on to hatred. Men hated the light (**3.20**) and the 'Book of Signs' showed how many of them came consequently to hate the One who was the light of the world. Jesus acknowledged that the world hated Him, though it could not hate His unbelieving brothers (**7.7**). But where His disciples are faithful, the hatred will spread to them (cf. **17.14**). The reason for the hatred was that He had picked them out from the world, and nobody likes a convert taken away from his own side.

Notes: V. 12: 'My commandment' is singular, perhaps summarizing all commandments (10). V. 13: there is no reason to suppose here that Jesus did not die for the whole world. It is His friends who specifically benefit from it and appreciate it. And it is by receiving His sacrifice for themselves that they become in a real sense His friends. V. 15: the contrast between servants and sons had been made in **8**.35. Here it is servants and friends. The friends need to do His will just as much as servants, but because they have a different relationship and a fuller knowledge, it is done on a different footing. V. 16: the friends of Jesus are not marked off by natural attractiveness nor even by their own moral choice. His sovereign will initiates and maintains the relationship.

St. John 15.20-27

The new relationship which Christ offers to His disciples is such that it makes all the more inevitable that they will stand alongside Him and share the world's reaction to Him. They have been called friends, but there is still a proverb about servants which fits their case. 'A servant is not greater than his master'. There will be identification, at least to some extent, with His fate. While the note of warning predominates—that there will be persecution—there is also a note of encouragement—that some, at least, will keep their words. Yet the emphasis seems to be on the adverse reaction, which happens for His sake, through people's failure to know God (**8.**19,55; **16.**3).

What is the root cause of sin? The Jews might have been able to make excuses for their sin had not the light come and shone in their midst, and had not the words and deeds of Jesus been witnessed by them. Their hatred of the light, their hatred of Jesus, was hatred of the Father. This is a hatred which fulfilled Scripture, being without any valid cause.

All this must be seen and understood in the light of the great new fact—the personal coming of the Holy Spirit. The Paraclete was to be sent by the Son from the Father. He was the Spirit of truth sent to combat the falsehood and unbelief in the world. It was one of the functions of the Holy Spirit to bear witness to Jesus. It was also the task of an apostle to bear witness to Jesus. They were qualified to do this because they had been with Him from the beginning of the ministry (cf. Acts **1.**21 f.) and were consequently able to testify to the truth of the apostolic preaching (*kerygma*) about Him. So we in our generation rely on this twofold witness— the historical witness of the apostles to the facts and their meaning, which by the inspiration of the Holy Spirit is recorded in the N.T., and the 'existential' witness of the Holy Spirit at work in the world today.

Notes: V. 20: see **13.**16. V. 21: 'on My account'—cf. Matt. **5.**11; **10.**22; Mark **13.**13. V. 22: for the Law also as a revealer of sin, see Rom. **7.**7 For the guilt of unbelief, cf. **9.**41. V. 25: '*their* law'— which they profess to belive in (cf. **5.**45–47). V. 26: there is no reason to suppose from this verse that the Spirit does not come from the glorified Son as well as from the Father (cf. **16.**7).

*For prayer: See Phil. **1.***12 ff. as an example of vs. 26 f., and pray for Christians who are being persecuted today.*

St. John 16.1-7

Jesus had been aware all along, not only of the presence of a traitor in the apostolic band, but also of the great weakness both in understanding and in character of those who sought to be loyal to Him. This teaching, He tells them, was to keep them from falling away. There were going to be many temptations for them to do that. Excommunication from the synagogue could be a powerful pressure on them. But things would go much beyond that. The time was coming when religious bigots, no doubt convinced in themselves of the rightness of their attitude, would do their best to kill them and really believe that this was something which was for the service of God. This was an attitude well illustrated by Saul of Tarsus who was convinced that he ought to act in the way that he did (Acts **26.**9–11). Jesus Himself was threatened with death on grounds of God's honour (**10.**31–33) as well as of the welfare of God's people (**11.**50). The reason for persecution of the Christians will be theological—lack of knowledge of Father or Son.

Jesus emphasizes that He is telling them things now which they did not need to know before when He was with them. These things must be said because of His imminent departure. They had not asked where He was departing to, but the fact that He was going had become a source of sorrow for them instead of one of joy (**14.**28). Paradoxical as it may have seemed to them it was for their benefit that He went. Without His departure the arrival of the Paraclete would be impossible. In view of what had already been said about the Holy Spirit, they should have realized how they (with all Christians who followed them) would be better off. So long as their love for Christ, their knowledge of Him and their joy in Him, were links to His physical life, they were vulnerable. Separation or death could destroy everything at a stroke. Now, 'nothing can separate us from the love of God in Christ Jesus' (Rom. **8.**39, cf. John **16.**22).

Notes: V. 2: cf. the threat of expulsion in **9.**22. There was a Jewish saying that 'everyone who sheds the blood of the godless is like one who brings an offering'. V. 4: cf. **13.**19, where such information would help them to believe in Him. V. 5: they had of course asked in **13.**36 and **14.**5 but they had become so involved in their own sorrow that they had not pursued the question further on this occasion. V. 7: ironically enough Caiaphas had seen the advantage of Jesus' going away (it is the same Greek word in **11.**50; **18.**14).

St. John 16.8-15

Jesus now expands upon the reasons why it will be advantageous to have the Holy Spirit. There is a great deal of concentrated teaching on the person and the work of the Spirit in these few verses. The first task of the Spirit is the threefold conviction of the world on the counts of sin, righteousness and judgement. This will be an exposure of the attitudes of the world in such a way as to touch the conscience of men. As the world cannot receive the Paraclete (**14.**17), it will, presumably, normally be effected through the witness of the apostles (**15.**26 f.). Counsel for their defence becomes through them counsel for the prosecution of the world.

It is interesting to note the substance of these charges. The charge of sin was connected not with wrong actions but with unbelief. The people of Israel had long ago been condemned for stifling the national conscience. God had given them prophets and Nazirites to remind them of His truth by their words and by their deeds, but they made the Nazirites drink wine and told the prophets not to prophesy (Amos **2.**11 f.). God's people had done the same again in refusing to accept the words and deeds of Jesus (**15.**22–24). The Spirit would show them also that they had the wrong idea of righteousness. True righteousness was the divine vindication of the righteous life of Jesus through the resurrection and ascension. Likewise with judgement. Despite all that was to follow, they could not judge Jesus. It was the devil and those who followed him who were judging and condemning themselves in the death of Christ.

In addition there was the teaching function of the Spirit. He would guide them into all the truth about Jesus. It would be His function to pass on to them all that Jesus wished to reveal, and so to bring glory to Him.

Notes: V. 13: this does not mean that the Holy Spirit guided the apostles or the Church into the fullness of truth about everything. It was a specific promise to those whose business it was to record, interpret and pass on the once-for-all events connected with Christ's ministry, death and resurrection. 'The things that are to come' may be specifically the cross and resurrection, rather than a general power of prediction.

St. John 16.16-24

Jesus now tells His disciples about their not seeing Him and then their seeing Him again. This will be in a little while. The disciples are puzzled and do not know what He means by the expression. Interpreters of the Gospel since have not been in much better case! The question is whether the two references to 'a little while' denote different periods of time. Some have suggested that within a few hours they would not see Him because of His death. Then a few hours later they would see Him again because of His resurrection.

More probably, both instances of the phrase refer to the brief period between cross and resurrection which was a time of not seeing but of being about to see Jesus again.

Because of their difficulty in understanding, Jesus gives them a short parable. The time will be one of sorrow for them and of joy for the world, but their sorrow will be turned into joy. For it is like the anguish of childbirth. This time of crisis is sorrowful but soon turns into joy with the advent of new life. So their brief, temporary sorrow would turn into deep and permanent joy. Then they would start to ask the Father things in His name. If they asked they would receive and their joy would be full.

Notes: V. 16: the seeing may not be altogether unconnected with the seeing of Christ in the end (1 John **3**.2). Seeing Him after the resurrection gives us a foretaste of the final vision. V. 17: the expression and reiteration of the doubt in this and in the next two verses suggest that some ambiguity may· have been intended. V. 21: this is not merely an illustration of any sorrow giving way to joy. In the O.T. the Messianic age was expected to be like childbirth, delivering God's people from their afflictions (Isa. **26**.16–20; **66**.7–14). Vs. 23 f.: there would be direct access to the Father, though prayer would be made in the name of Christ and on His authority, because of His effective work of reconciliation.

St. John 16.25-33

The circumstances of the ministry and the degree of understanding which the disciples have had have been such that Jesus has had to use a great deal of figurative language. The time would soon come when He would speak plainly of the Father. Not, of course, that it is possible to speak of divine truth without some use of human metaphor. But the possession of the Holy Spirit and the new degree of understanding which would come to the disciples would make much more direct teaching possible.

Jesus returns to the subject of prayer. After His exaltation, prayer would be made in His name. It would depend on His opening up of the way to the Father, but there would be no idea of the Son having to plead with an unwilling Father for the needs of His disciples. This would be unnecessary because of the Father's love for them. Their own love for and faith in Jesus were tokens that they were recipients of the Father's love. There was this close connection between attitudes to the Father and the Son because He Himself had His origin and destination with the Father, only being in the world for a time.

The disciples profess now to see the plain truth. They say that

72

they understand His supernatural knowledge and therefore His divine origin. But Jesus warns them that such belief will be tested 'soon. For they were about to be scattered and to desert Him. In the face of the assault of the world He offered them peace and the confidence that He had already won the victory. This would be, and still is, a proof of His claims.

Notes: V. 28: this may be, in very summary form, the plain truth which Jesus tells them. The reply of the disciples seems to suggest it. V. 31: the implication is of a completely inadequate faith. V. 33: for the cross and resurrection as victory over the powers of the world, cf. 1 Cor. **15**.57; Col. **2**.15.

Questions for further study and discussion on St. John chs. 15 and 16
1. 'Apart from Me you can do nothing' (**15**.5). What in fact do we do in Christian or other activity apart from Christ? What difference would there be if Christ were really called upon to direct and help us in it?
2. Ought we still to expect hatred from the world (**15**.18–20)? If it does come, what form is it likely to take?
3. What are the advantages which we have in our day as opposed to those who lived before the Holy Spirit was given (**16**.7)?
4. Is our joy full and can no one take it from us (**15**.11; **16**.22)?
5. How has Christ overcome the world and what difference does this make to our lives (**16**.33)?

St. John 17.1-8

After the final discourse with the disciples, Jesus now turns to speak to His Father. This is often called the 'High-Priestly Prayer', as Jesus, the great High Priest, consecrates Himself to His coming death through which He will make atonement for the sin of the world (cf. **1**.29). Yet there is a good deal more to the prayer than just this theme, for it deals with some of the great doctrines of the Gospel—the relationship of Father and Son (1–5), the relationship of the Son to the disciples and of the disciples to the world (6–19), and the relationship of the Son to later generations of believers and their relationship to the world (20–26).

The hour towards which the clock of destiny has been ticking throughout the ministry has now come. In the mind and will of Jesus His work is already finished (4). He has accepted the Cross and taken it upon Himself as the full and perfect expression of love. So now He asks His Father that it may be an occasion for the glory of both Father and Son (**13**.31 f.). The object of the Son's mission was to give eternal life in the knowledge of the Father and the Son. That mission had been accomplished and so had given glory to the Father. As it has been accomplished Jesus asks that He may now return to His Father and the glory which He had before the incarnation, and which had been His from the beginning before the creation of the world.

The mission of Christ was partly to make the name or character of the Father known to His disciples. They belonged to the Father and were given to the Son and they had been faithful. Now they also had knowledge of the divine origin and authority of Jesus.

Notes: V. 2: this is a strong reminder of the divine sovereignty. For the giving by the Father to the Son, cf. **3**.35; **6**.37–39; **10**.27–29. The last passage also speaks of giving eternal life to the disciples. V. 3: this is the only attempt in the Gospel at a definition of one of its leading concepts—eternal life. It is shown to be a personal relationship with God based on the historical mission of the Son, to know whom is to know God (**14**.7). V. 4: complete obedience to the Father's will was a characteristic of the ministry (**4**.34) and was sealed in His death (**19**.30). V. 6: the manifestation of the name or character of God was necessary for a true knowledge of Him which was not mere religious emotion.

St. John 17.9-19

Having described something of what He has done for the disciples, Jesus now turns to praying for them. He clearly distinguishes them from the world, for they belong in a special way to the Father and the Son. Because Jesus is leaving the world, their position as His representatives is of special importance. So He prays that His Father will keep them united and faithful. The unity of the disciples should be such as the unity of the Father and the Son. He also prays that they may have joy such as He had and would have in His return to the Father.

The passing on to them of the Word of God meant a calling of them out of the world. Their true allegiance was now elsewhere and they would therefore incur the hatred of the world. But He does not pray for their withdrawal from a hostile world but rather for them to be kept safe in the world from the attacks of the evil one. Just as Jesus Himself had a heavenly origin and destination, so in a sense the disciples have too. But just as He had a mission to the world, so have they. And His consecration of Himself was also a consecration of them for service.

Notes: V. 9: this does not mean that 'the world' is not still the object of God's love for whose sake the Son came (**3**.16). In the writings of John 'the world' means, not the created order as such, nor the gifts of God in nature and human life, but human life and society lived in disregard of God and under the power of evil. In the divine strategy the outreach to the world is always through the disciples (20 f.). Almost all prayer in the N.T. is prayer for Christians, but it includes the request that they should be ready to take evangelistic opportunities (cf. Acts **4**.29 f.). V. 10: cf. the dependence of the love of Christians (**15**.9) and their mission (**20**.21) on the relationship of the Father and the Son. V. 12: 'the son of perdition'—NEB, 'the man who must be lost' (cf. 2 Thess. **2**.3; 1 John **2**.18,22; **4**.3). In some sense he is almost an incarnation of Satan. Vs. 17,19: the consecration of the disciples for the service of God depends both on the truth of God's word (maybe a reference to Jesus Himself **1**.1; **14**.6) and on His consecration of Himself. It is not a mere human effort at self-improvement.

St. John 17.20-26

If the prayer had earlier been confined to the disciples as against the world (9), now it is extended to future generations of believers. The faith which they will have is expected to come through the word of the apostles. The prayer, for what will in due course become a very diverse company, is for their unity. It was to be a unity with its origin in the unity of Father and Son. It would be sustained by a continuing relationship to Father and Son and its object would be that the world should believe in the mission of the Son from the Father.

Even the glory which belonged to God is in some way passed on to the disciples to assist the perfection of unity and the demonstration to the world that they are recipients of God's love. So He prays that they may see His true glory. Because He has known the Father and they have known the mission of the Son, He has made the Father's name known to them and will continue to make it known. This revelation of the Father's character was to further their experience of the Father's love of the Son and deepen the Son's unity with them.

Notes: V. 20: His own mission to the world was to evoke faith in response to His word (**12**.47 f.). The apostles were to bring men to faith through the apostolic preaching (*kerygma*). V. 21: the reference is to a unity of will and purpose rather than one of organization. The dynamic relationship of Father and Son is the pattern. Mutual love and joint action are the best answer to this prayer, and when those are showing themselves, separate organizations will become irrelevant. It must never be forgotten that the object of Church unity is the glory of God and the evangelization of the world rather than administrative tidiness or comfort for Christians. V. 24: the disciples cannot fully follow yet (**13**.33,36) but there would be a foretaste of His glory before the full enjoyment of it (cf. Eph. **2**.6). V. 26: 'in them'—not only as individuals but in their midst also.

St. John 18.1-11

After three chapters of discourse and one of prayer, we come back now to action. But the Passion narrative in John, which we now begin to read, is different in emphasis from those of the other Gospels. Glory dominates. Even in the darkest moments there is triumph and victory. Jesus had warned His disciples about what was to happen, so that they would believe in Him (**13**.19). He had summoned them to rise and go out to the conflict (**14**.31). Now, after setting the coming affliction in the context of the whole plan of God and consecrating Himself and His disciples for this affliction and its consequences, He goes forth across the Kidron valley to a garden. Judas, having been identified and sent off to do his deed quickly, had gone out into the night (**13**.21–30). With the inner knowledge that he had from having belonged to the Twelve, Judas takes a band of Roman troops and Jewish temple police, and goes there to find Jesus.

Because of His foreknowledge of what was to happen, Jesus takes the initiative by coming forward and asking them whom they are seeking. To the reply 'Jesus of Nazareth' (His human designation) He replies, identifying Himself, but in terms which probably carried overtones of His deity, 'I am He' (cf. **6**.20; **8**.24,58)—a deduction supported by their immediate response in withdrawing and falling to the ground. When the question and answer are repeated, Jesus tells them to let the disciples go. The impetuous Peter draws his sword and cuts off the right ear of the high priest's slave. But Jesus rebukes this worldly attempt to frustrate His drinking the cup of suffering given to Him by His Father.

Notes: V. 1: 'a garden'. John alone describes it as such and does not name it as Gethsemane. Perhaps we are meant to see a conflict between Satan (**13**.27) and the Son of man, the second Adam. V. 3: religious and secular authorities combine against Him. 'A band' normally means a cohort of some six hundred soldiers. However, it is not necessary to presume that a force of this size

76

was used. Lanterns and torches were unnecessary to find the Light of the World (**8**.12) who was no longer hiding Himself (**12**.36; **18**.4). Weapons were unnecessary against One whose kingship was not of this world (**18**.36). V. 4: 'seek' may mean seek to kill (**5**.18; **7**.1, etc.). V. 5: Jesus is named as a Galilean (cf. **7**.52). Judas represents His own people—Judah (**1**.11; **4**.44). V. 6: this shows Jesus in command, willingly laying down His life (**10**.18). V. 8: He performs the part of the Good Shepherd and gives His life for the sheep (**10**.10–15).

St. John 18.12-18

Despite the willingness which Jesus has shown to be arrested, civil and religious authorities combine to seize Him and bind Him. They take Him first to Annas, father-in-law of Caiaphas the high priest. The evangelist reminds his readers of Caiaphas' attitude of cynical expediency to the execution of Jesus (**11**.49–52).

While Jesus goes alone as the prisoner, Simon Peter and another disciple follow. This disciple is known to the high priest so he manages to get into the court. Peter had stopped outside and has to be brought in by him. To a question from a maid whether he is one of Jesus' disciples the man of rock denies it. He then stands with the servants and officers trying to keep warm round a fire. He has denied the true light and stands with the enemies of his Master in the dark and in the cold.

Notes: V. 13: Annas was high priest from A.D. 6 to 15. Other references to him in the N.T. are in *Luke* and *Acts,* and both in conjunction with Caiaphas (Luke **3**.2; Acts **4**.6). He may have been the power behind the throne. Caiaphas (mentioned also in Matt. **26**.3,57) succeeded him after his deposition by the Romans and held the office until A.D. 36. There is some difficulty about this passage on the ground that there is no mention of a trial before Caiaphas (24,28) and Peter's denial comes into the examination before Annas. There is some very slight manuscript evidence for including v. 24 after 'Annas' in v. 13, but it is not strong enough to accept. Others have suggested that v. 24 has something of a pluperfect sense (as in AV [KJV]), stating that Annas *had* sent Him to Caiaphas. If we take the text as it stands it may be that there is no mention of a trial before Caiaphas because, in one sense, Jesus has nothing to say to such cynicism as Caiaphas had expressed (cf. Herod in Luke **23**.9). V. 15: it is natural to assume that this was the 'beloved disciple', but it is not certain. V. 17: 'I am not'—contrast the dignified reply of Jesus in v. 5. V. 18: standing with them, as

Judas had (5). How easily in our weakness we take the traitor's place!

St. John 18.19-27

The high priest begins his examination of Jesus, not by asking Him the basic questions about His origin and authority, but the more peripheral ones about His disciples and His teaching. Jesus has nothing to add to what He has already said in His public ministry. While He gave special teaching to His disciples at the Last Supper, His ministry was an open one. His message has been proclaimed in synagogue and Temple, places of public gathering. There is no point in His repeating it—His audience could tell them perfectly well.

Where argument fails, violence often takes over. An officer strikes Him but Jesus reminds them that the point at issue is the truth of His teaching and such a point is not solved in this way. Annas then sends Him bound to Caiaphas.

The scene switches back to Peter. Those with whom he has identified himself ask him if he does not in fact belong with the prisoner. For the second time he denies that he is a disciple. One of Malchus' relations then asks suspiciously whether he did not see Peter in the garden with Jesus. There is no glory here, only shame. For the third time Peter denies, and as Jesus predicted, the cock crows.

Notes: V. 19: certain questions are put to Jesus but hardly pursued. The decisions have been made secretly (not openly) without giving Him a fair trial (7.45–52). V. 20: Jesus' teaching has been done openly and to the world, though not in the way which His brothers had expected (7.3 f.). The word 'openly' could also mean plainly (16.29). But what was plain to His disciples would be hidden in meaning to the Jews, and even at this stage seems to have been lost on Peter. There is only one reference in the Gospel to His teaching in the synagogue (6.59). The main challenge to the Jews in their religious setting is made in the Temple. V. 21: the blind man had questioned the need to repeat his evidence. There was no possibility here of their wishing to become His disciples (9.27).

St. John 18.28-40

Jesus is sent from the religious leaders to the Roman governor; from the prejudiced judgement of His own people to the bewildered judgement of the world. With a supreme example of hypocrisy they refuse to run the risk of ritual defilement by entering Pilate's headquarters, though they are in the midst of defiling themselves morally (Isa. **59**.3). And in an amazing situation of irony they are preparing to eat the Passover without realizing that they are taking part in the putting to death of the true Passover Lamb in whose redemptive death the real significance of the festival is found.

To Pilate's tactful visit to them outside the praetorium and to his question about the charge which they brought, there is no reasoned answer. If He were not a criminal they would not have brought Him. Pilate wishes them to judge Him by their own law. But they say it is not lawful for them to put any man to death. They have determined that Jesus must die and die on a cross.

There is an inner stage as well as an outer. Inside the praetorium Pilate confronts Jesus and asks Him the question that matters as far as the Roman authorities are concerned. Are you the King of the Jews, a revolutionary leader? When Jesus tries to find out whether this is a conclusion Pilate has reached for himself, Pilate asks in desperation what on earth he could know about it all. What is this all about? Jesus puts the whole idea of kingship on to a different footing. Kingship, as Pilate knows it, is not the point at issue, it is truth. Outside Pilate has to face the demands of the Jews, inside he must face the claims of truth.

So Pilate with a despairing rhetorical question about truth, goes out in the cause of truth to tell the Jews that Jesus is innocent. But he wants to find a way around the problem and so makes use of the Passover amnesty. He has misjudged public opinion. They call out, not for Jesus their 'King' who was no threat to the Roman rule, but for a terrorist called Barabbas.

The way in which Jesus answered Pilate, and the things He did, are an example to all of us, and especially to Christians who are persecuted. Jesus renounced violent retaliation and even violent self-defence (36). His only weapons were supernatural and spiritual; so are ours (2 Cor. **10**.4).

Notes: V. 28: defilement would come by going into the house of a Gentile from which the leavened bread had not been removed. V. 31: their own law was in fact against them in their opposition to Jesus (**5**.45–47, cf. **7**.51). V. 31: it is uncertain whether the Jews had power to stone people at this time. V. 33: are *you* in all your weakness King of the Jews? V. 35: he feels quite out of it. The Gospel shows again and again that it is 'the Jews', 'His own people' (**1**.11) who are against Jesus. V. 37: 'Everyone who is of the truth'—cf. **3**.21.

To think over: 'Weakness is the only strength we have in presenting

*the gospel. And if you rob us of that we are going to get in real
trouble' (D. T. Niles).*

Questions for further study and discussion on St. John chs. 17 and 18

1. The word 'give' appears sixteen times in ch. **17.** What encouragement can we derive from the various ways in which it is used?
2. Mission, unity and truth are three major themes of ch. **17.**
What is the right order of priority for them?
3. 'Put your sword into its sheath' (**18.**11). How far is this a command to be obeyed on other occasions?
4. Do we ever deny our Christian discipleship by our words or by
the company we keep (**18.**17)? How can this be remedied?
5. What religious scruples do we fuss over while permitting harm
to others (**18.**28)?
6. 'What is truth?' (**18.**38). Are we prepared to face up to truth as it
challenges us at a personal level?

St. John 19.1-7

Having failed to get rid of the responsibility for dealing with Jesus
by means of an amnesty, Pilate now has Him flogged. This may be
an attempt to get Jesus to give evidence (cf. Acts **22.**24), or an
attempt to placate the Jews so that they would not go on asking for
the death penalty (Luke **23.**16,22). The soldiers then do their utmost
to humiliate this so-called king by mockery. They dress Him up in
royal robes and proceed to call Him 'King of the Jews' and to
strike Him.

Pilate goes out again in the name of truth on the level at which
he understands it, and tells the Jews that he finds no case against
Jesus (cf. **18.**38). Jesus then follows, a pitiful sight in His mock
array, and Pilate offers Him to their view telling them to look at the
man. Here is this poor fellow, your deluded and rejected Messianic
claimant, is what he means. But here is 'the Man', the Son of man,
the Second Adam, offering His perfect obedience for the life of the
world (Rom. **5.**15, 19; Phil. **2.**6–8).

The religious leaders see Him and howl for His crucifixion.
Pilate is still concerned enough for the truth not to be willing to
order the crucifixion. He has, however, given in sufficiently to the
pressure of the Jews to offer them the opportunity of performing it.
But they continue to call out for Pilate to act. The true charge now
comes out. It is a charge of blasphemy, which under Jewish law
carried the death penalty (Lev. **24.**16). The 'man' has made Himself Son of God (cf. **10.**33).

Notes: V. 2: the crown was probably not so much an instrument of torture as a symbol of mockery. It was probably a 'radiate crown' which was sometimes used as a sign of divinity. V. 3: see NEB—'Then time after time they came up to Him'. V. 4: the Jews themselves had been unable to prove any moral charges against Him (**8.46**). V. 6: the Jews could not crucify Him, so this may have been a taunt by Pilate. He is anxious to make them responsible for the execution. But this is a 'buck' which no man can pass.

St. John 19.8-16

Against the apparent hardness and moral unconcern of 'the Jews', Pilate is clearly set as a man who is trying to make up his mind, trying on the level at which he understands them to come to terms with the claims of the truth. So he is afraid. Partly afraid because the title 'Son of God' was one that the Roman emperors claimed and this, therefore, had a smell of treason about it. Partly afraid no doubt because the 'man' (5) showed so many signs of being more than an ordinary man.

Pilate therefore asks Jesus where He came from. This may be simply a matter concerned with jurisdiction (cf. Luke **23**.5 f.). But it is the all-important theological question (cf. **3**.31; **8**.23). Jesus does not reply to this direct question (cf. **8**.25). Pilate then reminds the prisoner of his authority—power to release and power to crucify. But this is no absolute power. It comes delegated from above, not so much from Rome as from God (Rom. **13**.1–7) and Pilate has not realized that Jesus has power to lay down and take up His life (**10**.18). Pilate is in a way only doing his job, the real sinner is the one who handed Jesus over.

Pilate, endeavouring again to release Jesus, makes another attempt to follow the claims of the truth. But the Jews have another weapon—insecurity. They have acted to preserve their interests against the temporal power (**11**.48–50). Now Pilate is reminded of his interests with the one who had on the earthly level given him power. This is sufficient to sway Pilate finally, for like most men he has his price. He brings Jesus out and sits down on the judgement seat. He then offers Him to them again, this time as their king. When they call for His crucifixion, Pilate asks incredulously, 'Shall I crucify your King?', and receives the terrible reply, 'We have no king but Caesar'. So do the people of God abandon their heritage. Nothing remains but to hand Him over to them for crucifixion.

The decisive shout of the priests (15) marks the end of the continual conflict in John's Gospel between light and darkness—the light and truth of Christ, and the darkness of the Jews. It is an ironic end. The Jews reject their King-Messiah, whom they cannot and will not recognize, by declaring their allegiance to an Emperor and an army of occupation which they hate. It is always the same. To reject Christ as King involves accepting or declaring allegiance to some other master, who will turn out to be empty and unsatisfying at best, and a tyrant at worst.

Notes: V. 11: the last phrase could refer either to Judas or to Caiaphas. Each represents Judaism as a whole with its claim to sight (**9.41**). V. 12: ironically, in the end Pilate was removed by Caesar. Just as ironically, the Romans ultimately came and destroyed the Temple (**11.48**). V. 13: Gabbatha has recently been discovered. V. 14: the day of Preparation might be the day before the Passover or the day before the Sabbath of Passover week. 'The sixth hour'—John probably used the Roman (and modern) time system.

St. John 19.17-22

The struggle between the two ideas of kingship is ended with apparent victory for the rulers of this world. The argument concerning the truth is over, with the One who is true falsely charged and sentenced, and the truth only shining out of the narrative unintentionally or ironically. The decision has been made on the human level and now comes the action.

Jesus went out carrying His own cross to Golgotha. There He was crucified with two others, who were possibly associates of Barabbas in his terrorist activity. So radically was Jesus misunderstood that they numbered the sinless One among the transgressors (Isa. **53**.12), they crucified One whose kingship was not of this world, and who abhorred the use of violence, between two violent criminals.

There must be a reason why a man should receive the sentence of crucifixion. Pilate, therefore, will have the last grim laugh. This is 'The King of the Jews'. So the title goes up in the three important languages of the day. Aramaic (rather than Hebrew) was the language of the Jews, Greek and Latin the official languages of the Empire. The message of the cross is proclaimed to His own people and to the world, of which He is the Saviour (**4.42**). So far as Pilate is concerned He is Jesus of Nazareth, a description such as any of his subjects might have. To that is added, in scorn of the whole business, the title of king. The Jews, who have just declared that they have no king but Caesar (15), naturally object. To show that

82

He was a false Messianic pretender would hurt no one, as this did. But Pilate stands firm and the title, unwittingly given remains. So in the end did they take Him by force to make Him King (**6.**15).

Notes: V. 17: 'bearing His own cross'. It is possible to harmonize this with Mark **15.**21. John is emphasizing that Jesus goes alone to accomplish the world's salvation. (Cf. also Isaac carrying the wood for his own sacrifice—Gen. **22.**6.) 'Golgotha'—the derivation of the name is uncertain and its location is not sure. V. 19: Pilate had already used this title five times. The Jews refuse to use it (cf. v. 12, 'a king'). In a sense it is a more limited title than 'the King of Israel' (**1.**49; **12.**13); and all the more ironic for the way in which 'the Jews' have been so opposed to Him in the Gospel. He is still King whatever men's response. V. 21: Jesus had, in fact, never said this.

St. John 19.23-30

To the soldiers Jesus is just another criminal to be dealt with, a political one with no very noticeable difference at the moment. So they carry on and collect the 'benefits' of the job—the prisoner's clothing. His tunic, the undergarment worn next to the body, was seamless and indivisible like that of the high priest (Exod. **28.**31 f.; Lev. **21.**10): there is no point then in trying to tear that. 'Let's toss for it,' they say. And so the soldiers, no doubt thinking of their good or bad luck in being on this 'job', commit themselves further to chance by gambling for the tunic. But there is no chance in the ways of God. This was to fulfil the Scripture, and in what a remarkable way, through the operation of those who did not know what they were doing, was Psa. **22** fulfilled in the Passion!

If the cross creates a false fellowship of gamblers trying to gain from the victim and from each other, it creates also a true fellowship of believers. Not only is there a group representative of the Church gathered around, but from the cross the word is spoken which puts Jesus' mother and the 'beloved disciple' into a new relationship with each other.

The mission of Jesus had been concerned with accomplishing the work which the Father had given Him to do (**4.**34). Here He knows that it has been accomplished, fantastic as this must have seemed to those who stood by. So He cries out, 'I thirst.' They come to meet His thirst on the physical level, so fulfilling the Scripture (Psa. **69.** 21). But His real thirst may be a spiritual one, for His Father (Psa. **42.**2). He who offers the living water, so that men need never thirst again (**4.**13 f.; **6.**35), Himself endures the agonies of thirst.

He who offers the Spirit and life (**7**.39) gives up His own spirit in death. Salvation does come to us freely, but not cheaply. The last cry from the cross (30) was one of triumph not of despair. He could die in peace. No one took His life. He gave it up freely, completing and perfecting His God-given mission.

Notes: V. 24: some have contrasted the divisions (literally 'tearings') of the Jews (**7**.43; **9**.16; **10**.19) with the untorn tunic and have seen it to be symbolic of the unity of the Church, but this seems rather remote. V. 25: the mother of Jesus had been dissociated from Him in **2**.4 because His hour had not yet come. Now it has come and she is associated with Him. Our Christian witness is transformed when we can discern His time. V. 29: 'hyssop' would not be a very suitable plant to hold up a wet sponge. A similar word means 'javelin': so NEB renders.

For meditation: 'The Cross is the blazing fire at which the flame of our love is kindled, but we have to get near enough to it for some of its sparks to fall on us' (Stott).

St. John 19.31-37

So the hour has come, the work has been completed and Jesus has died. But that is not after all the end of the matter. For there are religious consequences for the Jews and for the disciples. The Jews have been busy with their Passover observances and while they go through with the removal of a Messianic pretender they do not intend to slip up in their religious observance (cf. **18**.28). The Law had said that a hanged man's body should not remain all night upon the tree as that would defile the land (Deut. **21**.22 f.). The Romans liked to leave the bodies on the crosses as a grim warning to potential troublemakers. Because the next day was the Sabbath of the Passover the Jews asked for the bodies to be taken away before nightfall.

The Romans could not, of course, remove the bodies until the victims were dead. In such cases, as an act of mercy, their legs were broken to hasten their death. This was done in the case of the two terrorists. When they came to Jesus they saw that He was dead already. So there was no need to break His legs, and one of the soldiers, probably just to check that He really was dead, thrust a lance into His side and there came out a flow of blood and water.

There was a witness of this and he gives true evidence for the faith of the readers. It was clearly something of importance. On the one hand, it was firm evidence of His death, particularly important as there were heretics who denied that Jesus had ever died. On the other hand, water and blood are symbols in the Gospel. Water is applied for cleansing and new birth (**3.**5) and drunk for satisfaction (**4.**13 f.). The blood of the Son of Man must be drunk so that men may live (**6.**53–56). By what the soldiers did not do and by what they did they fulfilled Scripture.

Notes: V. 31: there is some doubt as to whether this means the day of preparation for the Passover or for the Sabbath. V. 34: Tasker, ad loc., quotes the medical evidence for what happened. Probably the two sacraments are in mind (cf. 1 John **5.**6,8). But the point is, as Barrett puts it, ad loc., that 'the real death of Jesus was the real life of men'. V. 35: this does not seem to be the 'beloved disciple'. V. 36: so revealing Jesus as the true Passover Lamb (**1.**29; cf. Exod. **12.**46; Psa. **34.**20). V. 37: quoting Zech. **12.**10, the whole context of which has bearing on the Passion.

St. John 19.38-42

While the fact of the burial of Jesus is mentioned as part of the apostolic preaching by Paul (1 Cor. **15.**3 f.), it is referred to very little in the N.T. As far as Paul is concerned it is probably only the link between death and resurrection which shows that both were real objective happenings. But John records a number of details about the burial which seem to have significance.

Joseph of Arimathea, a wealthy man and a member of the San-hedrin, comes and asks Pilate to be allowed to take away the body of Jesus. No doubt due to his influential position he obtains permission. So he does what the Jews want, and avoids the defilement of the land. But he is also a secret disciple of Jesus, so that, despite his fear of the Jews, this is an act of courage and is done in order to honour Jesus. Nicodemus, who has not yet been described as a believer but who was at least an open-minded sympathizer (**3.**1; **7.**50–52), joins with him. They take a huge quantity of spices and treat His body according to Jewish burial custom.

It is to a garden that they go with Him, for it is here that the Second Adam must bring life where the first Adam has brought sin and death (1 Cor. **15.**21 f.). It is a new tomb, perhaps prepared for the use of Joseph's family and now given to Jesus as no other can be prepared in time. Here, free from corrupting influences, He is laid—the first to lie in the tomb and soon to be the first to rise from the dead to a new sphere of life (1 Cor **15.**20). Despite the honour paid to Jesus by these two men, outwardly the victory belongs entirely to the Jews and to the forces of darkness. A dangerous pretender has been disposed of by the Romans, Barabbas has been freed and no one has even broken the Law!

Notes: V. 39: the immense weight of spices seems to echo Psa. **45**.8. V. 42: the NEB follows the Greek in making 'Jesus' the last word of the chapter. 'The future lies with Him, and with the Father' (Fenton, ad loc.).

Questions for further study and discussion on St. John ch. 19.

1. What pressures are there which come upon us today which might make us sin against the truth?
2. What does this chapter tell us of the claims of Christ in the spiritual and the temporal spheres?
3. How is it that the true kingship of Jesus is revealed in this chapter?
4. What effect does the cross have on our relationships with others (25–27)?
5. Does contemplation of 'Him whom they have pierced' (37) give us courage to act (38–42)?

St. John 20.1-10

The hand of legalism may seem to have triumphed as the drama must wait for a day while the Sabbath is observed. But after the Sabbath rest comes a new week and with it a new era in the history of mankind. Mary Magdalene comes to the tomb early, while it was still in every sense dark (cf. **13**.30; Luke **22**.53), but while dawn was imminent. She sees that the stone, such as would normally be placed across the entrance of a tomb to keep it safe, has been taken away. She naturally assumes that someone or other has violated the tomb and taken away the body of Jesus.

With this news she runs off to Peter and the 'beloved disciple'. The two of them then run as fast as they can to the tomb, and the 'beloved disciple', presumably the younger man, gets there first. He stoops to look into the tomb from the outside and sees the strange phenomenon of the graveclothes lying there. When Peter arrives he, as usual, is more impetuous and goes into the tomb. He sees the extra details—the different wrappings all lying in place. The boldness of Peter emboldens the 'beloved disciple' also, so he goes in and sees the evidence more closely and believes what has happened. This has come as a surprise because of their failure to know the Scriptural prediction that He should rise from the dead. So they go back home, thrilled no doubt but still mystified.

Notes: V. 1: Mary Magdalene was presumably not alone ('*we* do not know', 2), but is probably mentioned as the leader of the group of women and the one to whom the Lord appears personally (11–18). It is a forgiven sinner who makes the first discovery of the empty tomb and sees the first appearance of the risen Lord. V. 2: she probably thought of the enemies of Jesus, but the rifling of tombs was a fairly common crime. V. 7: Lazarus came out of the tomb with the wrappings still on him (**11.44**.) This was resurrection of a different kind, in which the form of the body seems to have been changed, so that it could slip out of the graveclothes without disturbing them. No one removing the body would have left the wrappings. V. 8: this is the first true Christian faith in the Gospel, because it is faith in the risen Lord. For an adequate confession we have to wait until v. 28.

St. John 20.11-18

If in a sense the 'beloved disciple' has come to Christian faith because he believes in the resurrection, it is Mary who comes to the first full Christian experience because she meets the risen Lord. For the fact of the empty tomb and the encounter with the risen Christ are the twin bases of the Easter faith.

As the Lord had gone, there was no point in staying at the tomb as far as the men were concerned. But somehow they had not communicated this to Mary. She remains weeping at the tomb as it was the place with which her Lord had last been associated, and she did not now know where to look for Him. Eventually she looks into the tomb and sees two angels. When they ask her why she is weeping she answers purely on the human plane. He has been moved from there and she does not know where they have put Him.

Turning round she sees the risen Jesus but does not recognize Him. To His question about the reason for her tears, she continues in the same vein of trying to discover where the dead Jesus is. Only the use of her name, no doubt in a familiar intonation, makes her realize that it is Jesus. Her apparent desire to cling to Him is forbidden. He must ascend to His Father. She must go and tell His brothers about this. So she goes off to the disciples, His newly-made brothers in the Christian family, and tells them that she has seen the Lord.

Notes: V. 12: it may be that she needed the evidence of the angels which was not needed by Peter and the other disciple. V. 15: a very different kind of seeking from **18.4**,7. V. 16: the Good Shepherd calls His own sheep by name (**10.3**). It helps us to think of Him

using our names. 'Rabboni' is an inadequate confession of faith
(cf. 28). V. 17: she may have touched Him (cf. 27). She was not to
cling to His body in this state because His abiding presence after
the ascension would be a spiritual one (14.18). 'My Father and your
Father'—they are brothers (cf.1.11) but His relationship to the
Father is still unique(1.14).

St. John 20.19-23

The disciples have now heard of the empty tomb, which some of
them at least have seen for themselves. They have also heard of the
appearance of Christ to Mary Magdalene. But they have not yet
met the risen Lord for themselves. To them the experience of the
Easter faith comes not at the tomb nor in the garden but in a room
where doors are shut through fear of the Jews.

Jesus passes through closed doors and greets them with a message of peace, now filled with new and wonderful meaning for them
(cf. 14.27). The evidence that He really is Jesus has to come not only
from His words but also from His body. The marks of crucifixion
are displayed to them. No wonder the disciples were filled with joy
(16.20–22). Jesus then repeats His word of peace and commissions
them for mission in His name. He breathes on them and imparts the
Holy Spirit to them. Their mission and the gift of the Holy Spirit
through which alone they could accomplish it (cf. Acts 1.8) are
connected with the forgiveness and the retention of sins.

Notes: V. 19: it is important to emphasize that this appearance to
the representative body of the disciples was on the first day of the
week, the first day of the new era. For fear of the Jews, cf. 7.13;
19.38. The emphasis here seems to be more on the power of Jesus
in His 'spiritual body' to pass through closed doors and yet be
recognized, than on the disciples' fear. But we can see how frigh-
tened men were transformed in preparation for their fearless mission to the world. It is not certain whether only the Twelve (minus
Thomas and Judas) were in the room. If this is so, then they are
there as representatives of the Church as a whole. V. 21: the mission
of the disciples from the Son is derived from and parallel to the
mission of the Son from the Father (cf. 17.18). V. 22: this is sometimes referred to as the 'Johannine Pentecost'. Jesus can impart the
indwelling Holy Spirit as soon as He has risen, though the full outward manifestation of the gift of the Spirit to the Church must wait
until the appearances are over. There is here a new creation (cf.
Gen. 2.7). The Second Adam is a lifegiving Spirit (1 Cor. 15.45).
V. 23: the forgiveness or retention of sins is the inevitable result

of men's reaction to the Gospel. What happened in His ministry (**9**.39–41) will happen in them through the Holy Spirit (cf. **16**.8–11).

St. John 20.24-31

For some reason Thomas had not been present when Jesus appeared to the disciples on the evening of Easter Day. When the disciples tell him of the resurrection experience in the simplest terms—'We have seen the Lord' (cf. 18)—Thomas asks for more detailed evidence by sight and by touch before he will be convinced.

A week later comes the answer for Thomas. Again Jesus passes through closed doors and again He gives them His greeting of peace. Then He invites Thomas to put the evidence for the resurrection to the test which he had wished to make for it. It seems that touch was not necessary, the evidence of sight was sufficient. Thomas cries out in adoring wonder, 'My Lord and my God!'

The Gospel has reached its climax. An adequate confession of faith has at last been made, Jesus is confessed not only as Lord (cf. Rom **10**.9; 1 Cor. **12**.13), but also as God (cf. **1**.1). Thomas' faith has been based on sight. But Jesus is concerned about those who will believe in later generations and in different places (**17**.20). So He pronounces His last beatitude upon those who will not have the privilege of sight but who will exercise the gift of faith.

As the climax has been reached the evangelist rounds off his work. He reminds his readers that the signs recorded are only a selection of all that Jesus did, and that they are selected for a purpose—to induce a faith in Jesus as Christ and Son of God which will bring life.

Notes: V. 24: Thomas, as shown earlier (**11**.16; **14**.5), seems to have been loyal but to have lacked the perception of faith. V. 28: 'My Lord' contains much fuller meaning than Mary's expression of the same words in v. 13. Paradoxically, it is the doubter who in the end expresses his faith most completely. May our honest doubts find a similarly complete answer! V. 31: it is probably a present rather than an aorist. This would mean 'hold the faith' (NEB) rather than 'come to believe' (NEB margin). The Gospel would therefore be intended for Christians as well as non-Christians.

St. John 21.1-8

The Gospel proper ends with ch. **20**. This chapter is a sort of appendix, the particular purpose of which is apparently to explain what Jesus had said about the destiny of the 'beloved disciple' (23).

It also has importance in showing the manner of Peter's restoration to the service of Christ, and the future which awaited him. So the relationship between Peter and the 'beloved disciple' is made clear. Both are represented as equal partners with complementary roles—Peter as pastor and evangelist, and the beloved disciple as guarantor of the truth concerning Jesus (25). These two leaders were obviously the subject of widespread rumours (23).

There were a number of different appearances to the disciples by the risen Lord (see 1 Cor. **15**.3–8) not all of which are recorded in the Gospels. As always, John has selected one which gets across an important point (**20**.30 f.; **21**.25). The disciples had apparently gone back to Galilee, uncertain of the way in which they were to carry out the apostolic commission (**20**.21). Seven of them are mentioned. Simon Peter decides to go fishing and the rest follow his lead.

Night was the best time for fishing, but a hard night's toil yielded nothing. At daybreak Jesus, unrecognized, asked them from the shore whether they had any fish. When they said they had not He told them to cast their nets to starboard. They made such a catch that they could not haul it in. The 'beloved disciple' is the very first to discern who the stranger is. But it is Peter who acts first, putting on his clothes and plunging into the lake while the others struggled in with the boat and the catch. Both types of people are found in the Church today. When they work together the cause of Christ prospers.

Notes: V. 1: the Sea of Tiberias was the same as the Sea of Galilee. V. 2: Thomas is prominent in *John*, Nathanael is mentioned only by him. This is the only reference to the sons of Zebedee in the Gospel and it helps us to assume that John was the 'beloved disciple'. But this is not certain, for it could possibly have been one of the two unnamed disciples. V. 6: Jesus probably saw a shoal of fish from the shore. It is not at all certain how far this story is meant to have symbolic significance with 'fishing for men' being illustrated (cf. Luke **5**.10 f.). V. 7: 'the Lord'—it is only after the resurrection that the disciples are recorded as referring to Jesus by this title in the third person.

St. John 21.9-14

Eventually all the disciples arrive, following Peter. They find that Jesus has already been at work. He has made a fire upon the shore and has cooked some fish and provided some bread. Jesus asks them to bring some of the fish which they themselves have caught and Peter goes back to the boat and hauls the net ashore. In it there were one hundred and fifty-three fish but the net was not torn.

Jesus then asks them to have breakfast with Him. There is about Him a numinous quality which stops them from asking who He is, but, in fact, they knew without having to ask that it was the Lord. In any event He can cope with shyness. He came and took and distributed both bread and fish as He had done to them and the five thousand beside the same lake before (**6.**11). It was in a meal, which must have reminded them of meals which they had shared with Him, as well as of the feeding miracle, that He revealed Himself. Luke too shows that 'He was known to them in the breaking of the bread' (Luke **24.**28–35). So in this informal fashion was Jesus revealed to them for the third time after He was raised from the dead.

Notes: V. 10: it is not clear why Jesus asked them to bring their fish when He had already prepared some for them to eat. It appears that their fish was not used on this occasion. V. 11: this number has long exercised the ingenuity of commentators. It may simply be that they counted up and this happened to be the total. But many have seen it to be symbolic. Some suggest that it represents the one hundred and fifty-three different species of fish known to ancient naturalists, or that, as factorial seventeen, it symbolizes perfection (as ten and seven were numbers indicating completeness). In either case this would be taken as referring to the complete apostolic mission to all men which would be carried out by the Church without the nets breaking. However, the primary meaning of the whole chapter must undoubtedly be sought on the plain literal level. V. 12: 'Who are You?'—this was the question the Jews had put to Him in unbelief (**8.**25). V. 13: while it would be wrong to see this as a celebration of the Holy Communion, our doctrine of the Lord's Supper should include the idea of eating together with the risen Jesus in our midst.

St. John 21.15-19

Simon Peter has been the leader of the band of the disciples. He has not always believed first (**20.**8) nor perceived first (7), but he has usually acted first. And through being in a prominent position it is he who has denied his Master three times. He has already hastened ashore to meet Jesus and it is clear that he wishes to put right his denial. First they eat the meal of fellowship and then Jesus takes the initiative in restoring Peter.

Three times Peter had denied that he knew Jesus (**18.**15–27), and now three times Jesus asks him if he loves Him. It was only in reply to Peter's threefold assurance that he did love Him that Jesus gave him the threefold commission to feed His lambs and His sheep. At the third question Peter is upset, but Jesus reminds him as He had done before (**13**.6–10) of his need for submission. When he was young he had the independence and opportunities of youth. When he was old things would happen to him against his will. This was a prediction of a martyr's death, in which he would glorify God as his Master had done before him (**12**.23–26). This was to be his destiny; it was for God's glory, it was the way Jesus had gone. So the command comes, and echoes down the centuries, 'Follow Me'.

Notes: Vs. 15–17: despite NEB margin, most scholars do not now try to distinguish between the two words used for 'love' in these verses. John often uses synonyms and there is no reason to suppose that he is recording reference to love at two levels—the word used by Jesus in vs. 15 f. referring to Christian love, and the word used by Peter in vs. 15 f. and by both of them in v. 17 to human affection. Likewise there seems to be no real distinction between 'feed' (15, 17) and 'tend' (16), nor between 'lambs' (15) and 'sheep' (16 f.). It was to this pastoral ministry that Peter, in fact, devoted himself (1 Pet. **5**.1–5). 'More than these' refers to the other disciples (cf. Mark **14**.29), rather than to his love of the trappings of the fisherman's life. Peter has learnt enough humility not to make the comparison in reply. V. 18: this is important early evidence for the crucifixion of Peter.

St. John 21.20-25

It is always interesting to know what is going to happen to other people too. Human nature being what it is, we enjoy comparisons with others so that we can exult in our own virtue or grumble about our own misfortunes. Sometimes we wish to find out about others from sheer curiosity. Whatever the motive, Peter wants to know what is to happen to the 'beloved disciple'. Jesus answered that that is none of Peter's business, but puts it in such a way that He seems to predict that that disciple would not die before the second coming of Christ. The writer wishes to make it quite plain that Jesus did not say that but only 'If it is My will that he remain until I come, what is that to you?'

The book ends with the assertion that it is this disciple who is bearing witness to all this and has written this, and that it is known that his evidence is true. And in a charming concluding sentence the writer adds that if all the deeds of Jesus were recorded the world would not be large enough to hold all the books which should be written.

Notes: V. 20: it is not clear why such a long description is given of the 'beloved disciple'. It may be to contrast this incident with the other (**13.**21–30), when it seemed of considerable importance to both Peter and the 'beloved disciple' to know who was going to be the traitor. V. 22: perhaps this was deliberately expressed as the most different thing that could possibly happen to him, without any necessary implication that it would. V. 23: it is possibly necessary to state this because the 'beloved disciple' has recently died. If this is so, he is the witness behind the Gospel and the one responsible for its writing. Ch. **21** (or at least the last two verses) would then be edited by the disciples of the 'beloved disciple' ('we' in 24).

*A final thought: While ch. **21** may be something of a postscript to the Gospel, it is a most appropriate one. The transformation of an individual by Christ, through a personal encounter involving faith in Him, is what the whole Gospel is about.*

Questions for further study and discussion on St. John chs. 20 and 21

1. Compare the resurrection narrative in *John* with that in the other Gospels. Do the differences make the event seem more or less true?
2. Is belief in the empty tomb necessary for Christian faith?
3. In what way can we today meet the risen Lord personally?
4. 'Do you love Me?' Do we let Jesus ask us this question before we seek to do things in His service (**21.**15–17)?
5. Do we face the temptation of being more concerned with other people's progress than with following Christ ourselves (**21.**21 f.)?